THE WORLD GOES NOT WELL, BUT...

# THE KINGDOM COMES

THE WORLD GOES NOT WELL, BUT...

# THE
# KINGDOM
## COMES

~

DAVID R. MAINS

MAINSTAY MINISTRIES

*1-800-224-2735*

**The Kingdom Comes**
Copyright © 2019 by David R. Mains

First printing, 1983; reprinted, 2005
Revised and reprinted in 2019 by Mainstay Ministries in the United States of America

ISBN 978-1-942364-33-7

---

Cover Design, Meridith Albert, Arizona
Interior Design, JM Vergara, Philippines
Editor, George Koch, Illinois
Publisher, Randall Mains, Texas

Published by Mainstay Ministries
West Chicago, Illinois
www.SundaySolutions.com
1-800-224-2735

*Dr. David R. Mains uses key passages of Scripture to explain the Kingdom truths that undergird the immensely popular Tales of the Kingdom Trilogy he and his wife, Karen, wrote.*

*Dedicated to our son,*
*Randall John,*
*through whose efforts*
*The Kingdom Tales*
*have been kept alive*
*through many decades.*

# TABLE OF CONTENTS

~

# FOREWORD

~

T*HEIR CONVERSATION WAS INTERRUPTED by a cry that echoed through the woods: "How goes the world?"*
*The answer came back: "The world goes not well."*
*Then another answer. "The Kingdom comes."*
*"That's the Watch cry," Amanda explained.*
*"It goes from tower to tower..."*

That short quote is from "The Faithless Ranger," story four in our book *Tales of the Kingdom*.

When we travel in meetings, it is also the way friends often greet us. This has happened enough times that we are now always prepared. If asked, "How goes the world?", our practiced response is, "The world goes not well." And then together, greeters and responders all say, "But the Kingdom comes!" Then more-normal conversation takes place.

For us, the thirty-six stories in our Tales trilogy are more than good children's literature. They were written to underscore for children of all ages basic truths regarding the primary teaching of our Lord. To our amazement, it is a message that is not understood all that well even by many in the Church.

We were sitting in an airport, waiting for the announcement that our plane was to begin boarding.

"David and Karen Mains?" someone asked.

"That's right!" we answered, turning to see a man approach us.

"The David and Karen Mains with the *Chapel of the Air* broadcast?"

"Uh-huh."

"I listened to your program. I liked it when you used Shakespeare in your messages. Are you students of Shakespeare?"

"Some. How about yourself?"

"Me too. That's why I said something. I thought I'd enjoy chatting for a few minutes. Uh, which of his plays have you most enjoyed reading?"

"Well," we responded, "We've never actually read any of his plays."

"Of course, of course—many people haven't. They were written to be performed. Which one have you enjoyed most on the stage?"

"Well, we said, "We're students of Shakespeare—but not his plays."

In amazement, the stranger asked, "How can you be students of Shakespeare and not know any of his plays? I mean, what's Shakespeare apart from his works?"

"Never thought of it that way," we confessed. "But we've studied his life."

"That's crazy," said the stranger. "I mean, when someone says he's a student of Shakespeare, one just assumes—"

But enough. The absurdity of this make-believe conversation is already obvious. But in Christian circles, unfortunately, a similar ridiculous discussion might take place.

"I understand you're a student of the teacher Jesus?"

"I don't know that a student is what I'd call myself—maybe a modern-day disciple."

"But that's what the word *disciple* really means—student—a student of a teacher."

"Oh, I didn't know that!"

"Well, as a modern disciple, what do you think of Jesus' message about the Kingdom of God?"

"I guess I'm … uh … not sure I've ever read that one."

"Not sure you've read it? What else did Jesus preach about besides the Kingdom?"

"Well, He talked about being born again."

"But that's simply to enter the Kingdom. 'Except a man be born again, he cannot enter the kingdom of God.' Study the New Testament. The Kingdom of God is its major theme! How can you be a disciple and not know about His dominant message!"

But again, my point is obvious.

This book attempts to put into simple terms a magnificent message that needs to be rediscovered by many modern-day students of the teacher Jesus.

Christ's disciples have been given the privilege of knowing the truths of His Kingdom. What an honor!

~

*The Ranger cry sped through Deepest Forest. "How goes the world?"*

*"The world goes not well…"*

*"But the Kingdom comes! … The Kingdom comes!"*

*All knew, from the littlest to the largest, that the King was now well and the Kingdom intact. They went about their work with glad hearts as the birds greeted the dawn.*

**From the *Tales of the Kingdom* story:**
**"The Baker Who Loved Bread"**

CHAPTER 1

# GOD'S ANOINTED KING

⤳

I N THE UNITED STATES we don't expect a great and godly president
to take office someday and establish a perfect government. No Scriptures
are quoted in our churches regarding such a figure. A prediction like this
has not been articulated by ancestral prophets and handed down through
the generations.

In New Testament times, however, just such a hope consumed the
hearts and minds of devout Jews. Like righteous old Simeon and Anna in
the second chapter of Luke. Such people looked for their *Messiah* with keen
anticipation. That term means "God's anointed one." Since Jewish kings
were themselves anointed with oil, the phrase "Anointed of the Lord" was
synonymous with the idea of kingship. And the Jews understood that the
great anointed one—the Messiah—would be a special king, anointed and
approved by God.

This is in contrast to other ancient cultures in which *all* kings were
viewed as gods. Roman emperors, for example, demanded worship from
their subjects; Egyptian pharaohs were regarded as divine incarnations; and
Babylonian monarchs were seen as links between the deities and mortals.
But no evidence of anything like this exists in early Jewish thought.

Although some of Israel's rulers tried to act like gods, the Jews' strong
messianic hope concerning the super-king fostered a painful awareness that
ordinary kings would always be incapable of meeting Jewish expectations.

But here's the point. When reading the New Testament, we see Christ
today filling many roles. He is our Savior, teacher, shepherd, healer, and
so on. Because of our kingless culture, however, we tend to downplay this
matter of the keenly anticipated messiah, or great anointed king. But it's
very important.

In John 1:43-51 Philip tells Nathanael, "We've found him of whom Moses wrote, Jesus of Nazareth." Nathanael responds somewhat sarcastically, "Can anything good come out of Nazareth?" But later, Jesus tells Nathanael, "Before Philip called you, when you were under the fig tree, I saw you." Dumbfounded because he knew Christ had not been there to see him, Nathanael replies, "Rabbi, you are the Son of God, you are the King of Israel."

Do you understand the significance of Nathanael's words? He was saying, "So, it's in you that our great hope for the perfect king is to at last be realized, our longing for the fulfillment of God's promise!"

For the early Church, the man Jesus and the Jewish hope for a long-awaited anointed king were literally fused into one! Like the Hebrew word *messiah*, the word *Christ*—from the Greek *christos*—also means "Anointed." The name *Jesus* and the title *Christ* were so locked together that they became a double name—*Jesus Christ*, or *Jesus the one anointed*. And the New Testament writers wanted their readers to be aware of this fact. Matthew, for instance, begins his gospel with the genealogy of Jesus Christ—or Jesus the anointed ruler.

Matthew establishes the fact that in our Lord's veins flowed the blood of the kings—David, Solomon, Rehoboam, Abijah, Asa, Jehoshaphat, and others—right through to the last of the kings of Judah.

In the second chapter of Matthew, when the wise men come from the East and ask, "Where is he who has been born king of the Jews?", Matthew quotes the prophecy from Micah about Bethlehem: "From you shall come a ruler who will govern my people Israel."

This king-consciousness doesn't stop with the gospels or in the region of Palestine, either. In Acts 17, while Paul is in far-off Thessalonica, the citizens are up in arms. They scream, "These men who have turned the world upside down have come here also and they are acting against the decrees of Caesar, saying that there is another king, Jesus."

By the end of the New Testament, the emphasis has only intensified. In Revelation, John writes, "I saw heaven opened, and behold a white horse! He who sat upon it is called faithful and true. On his robe and on his thigh he has a name inscribed, King of Kings and Lord of Lords."

In my Bible, on the first page of the New Testament, I have written these words: "I am reading about the greatest of all kings." Time and again before looking into God's Word I have turned to this sentence just to remind myself of the magnitude of what I'm doing. I'm reading about the greatest of all kings. I dare not overlook this.

The Jews of Christ's day—with all their misunderstanding of His Kingdom—were absolutely correct in being on the alert for a king who would establish a kingdom. To understand Christ's Kingdom, we too must recapture this same Jewish sense of expectation. Let me repeat that:

*To truly understand Christ's Kingdom, we must recapture this Jewish expectation of a promised king who was to reign.*

If we agree that Christ is a king, it follows next that what a king is expected to talk about most is his kingdom. What dominates a president's conversation? Not sports, photography, religion—no! He talks about his administration, his government. In this same way, Christ, as the long-awaited Messiah, the anointed king of Israel, talked about His reign, his kingship, his Kingdom—by necessity. If He hadn't, He wouldn't have been fair to His followers.

Luke 8:1 reads, "He went on through cities and villages preaching and bringing the good news of the kingdom—the kingdom of God." To miss this emphasis is to pass right over what Bible scholars agree is our Lord's basic message—His word about His Kingdom.

Why then are so many people ignorant of this—even good church people? Why are so many Christians unable to define the Kingdom? Perhaps you have been a Christian for years, but you're just not captivated by Kingdom talk or Kingdom dreams. Hearing a question like "How is the Kingdom of God progressing?" is like being asked about computer programming.

Maybe you've never been comfortable with the idea of Christ as your King. Perhaps kneeling has always seemed a bit awkward, and the only crown you've ever pictured Christ wearing was the one made of thorns. To address Him as "my sovereign" would make you feel extremely awkward.

Well, as we examine this topic, let's put on some Kingdom "study glasses." As you read Scripture, pretend you are putting on special glasses designed to help you spot every word, every phrase that relates to this king and his kingdom. I've already mentioned some of the words to watch for:

*Messiah, Christ, kingdom, ruler, govern, crown, sovereign,* etc. Together we will hunt for words like these in the New Testament. I believe you'll be amazed by how dominant this emphasis is!

Though it will help to remind yourself, as I wrote in my Bible, that you are reading about the greatest of all kings, that's not enough. You will need to make frequent use of your "Kingdom glasses." And as you study the Scriptures, try to recapture that Jewish expectation of a great king who was to reign—not just a great king, but a real king who is to reign over a real kingdom. Let's rediscover the world's greatest king and the world's greatest kingdom—of which all who believe in Christ are a part, whether they know it or not. But how much better to be aware!

~

*"There is a King," his mother had always insisted. "A real King." She believed the ancient tales even though signs were posted all over Enchanted City:*
*THERE IS NO SUCH THING AS A KING.*
*DEATH TO PRETENDERS!*
*But his mother had become ill, as so many did in the foul air of Enchanted City. In the last days before she died, she slipped in and out of the fever—often telling Scarboy the ancient tales from her childhood.*

**From the *Tales of the Kingdom* story:**
**"The Enchanted City"**

# CHAPTER 2

# The Pretender

~

ALL POSITIONS OF RANK have certain disadvantages. One of the headaches of kingship, for instance, is having to deal with the kingdom's enemies. At least this was true for the greatest of all kings.

We don't know the extent of the uprising, but we do know there was a rebellion in heaven that profoundly affected our planet. From it arose a pretender to the throne that is rightfully held by God's appointed King. Beautiful, intelligent and strong, this upstart is also devious; he is the very epitome of evil. The Bible pictures him as a great dragon. So threatening was this enemy, in fact, that even the King himself came to our planet, in the words of 1 John 3:8, to (catch the word) "Destroy the works of the devil."

The feeling was reciprocal, of course. No sooner had the King arrived on earth than His parents had to flee with Him from the destroyer. As early as Matthew 2 we see Satan's manipulations; God's angel warned Joseph to "flee to Egypt for Herod is about to search for the [Christ] child to [here's the word again] destroy him."

We who are servants of the King are also targets. "The thief comes," said Jesus, "Only to steal and kill and to [one more time now] destroy."

Here then is a fact all Christians must come to grips with. An evil personality has made his presence known in our world and has set himself up in opposition to our King. Some day this dark figure will become incarnate as a man—the Antichrist. It's a frightening thought, isn't it?

It reminds me of J. R. R. Tolkien's three-volume fantasy *The Lord of the Rings*, in which the dark cloud of Sauron is on the move, enveloping greater and greater portions of Middle Earth. To counter this force, an intrepid little band of warriors is chosen to defeat this sinister enemy. They are to infiltrate the stronghold of the evil lord himself and destroy the master ring of power in the great cracks of doom where it was first forged.

Sound overdramatic? If it does, then perhaps we are at the opposite extreme—totally unaware that our world is in fact a real battleground between two great spiritual powers.

In church we talk a lot about personal spiritual growth. But do we realize we are also involved in something much larger than personal growth? That is why I prefer to regularly use kingdom terminology: It makes us instantly aware that we are involved in a war of superpowers.

Do you realize that a dark cloud is on the move over our earth as well? To call oneself a Christian and ignore this truth is to operate out of a framework other than Christ's. He clearly saw we are involved in a massive clash of kingdoms, a struggle of light versus darkness, good against evil, righteousness battling sin, life overcoming death, and God defeating Satan.

And this is as true in our own individual lives as it is on the world scene. Don't misunderstand. What I'm referring to is not make-believe or merely doctrinal. It is literal.

The greatest personal source of help we have, of course, is our King. He teaches us and opens our eyes to reality. Referring to Satan, Jesus said, "He was a murderer from the beginning, and has nothing to do with the truth, because there is no truth in him. When he lies, he speaks according to his own nature, for he is a liar and the father of lies!"

Understanding the nature of His adversary, Jesus is downright blunt when Satan calls on Him after the long forty-day fast in the wilderness. The devil, seeing Christ's hunger, acted as though he sympathized: "If you're the Son of God, why don't you command these stones to become loaves of bread?"

Do you know any people who lie? Do you remember how closely you have to watch your words when you suspect someone is not being sincere? Well, I imagine Jesus felt that way toward the tempter. Jesus is guarded and His answers are crisp. He is careful, anxious not to get involved in an extended conversation.

"It is written," Jesus quotes from the Old Testament, "man shall not live by bread alone, but by every word that proceeds from the mouth of God."

In typical fashion, Satan doesn't give up. Next he suggests that Christ just kind of float down from the pinnacle of the temple in Jerusalem. And he quotes part of Psalm 91: "He will give his angels charge over you."

"Again it is written," responds Christ, more than dubious of any suggestion Satan would make, "You shall not tempt the Lord your God."

Finally—the real bottom line—Satan promises the glory of the kingdoms of the world if Christ will only fall down and worship him. The offer was surely phony to begin with. Satan is notorious for promising the moon, but what he delivers always falls short of what he advertised.

But Jesus wasn't about to be conned. He knew the character of the one with whom He was dealing. "Begone, Satan!" were His words.

Do you know what I think? Christians today need to develop more of this kind of wisdom regarding our enemy. We do well to realize that Satan has multitudes in his service, and they will attempt to derail us at every turn. In a sentence:

*It is mandatory that the followers of the anointed King be wise regarding the Kingdom's enemy.*

"We're not ignorant of his designs," wrote Paul to the Corinthians. And to the Ephesians he warned: "Put on the whole armor of God, that you may be able to stand against the wiles of the devil"—in other words, look out for his sly tricks and deceit!

Not that we should talk or think about the enemy that much or study up on him—we shouldn't be obsessed by the subject of Satan. But we shouldn't be naïve either. Jesus paid little attention to Satan or his hordes. Although Jesus cast out demons, He was not intrigued by them. To Him they were the enemy in a life-and-death struggle, who by their own choice had refused reconciliation. We would do well to emulate our Lord in this regard, to be aware of the enemy but have as little as possible to do with him or anything that represents him.

Let me illustrate what I mean by that last phrase, "Anything that represents him." You know what a skunk smells like, don't you? Suppose you were walking and saw one not far away. Would you try to establish a relationship with it? Call it over as you would a dog or a cat, "Here, pretty little skunk"? Would you pet it? Hardly!

I believe Christians need to have a "skunk" response to our enemy. We're not stupid, and we certainly respect what he can do. But we're anxious not to get in a spot where he can demonstrate his potency.

I wish I could endow believers with a keen sense of "spiritual smell" so we could sniff out the devil's presence by his stench every time he tries to get between us and the Lord. Perhaps while watching something questionable on television, we might say, "Oh, that seems rather interesting," then *(sniff, sniff, sniff)*, "Uh-oh—something stinks around here!" Being warned, we turn the set off.

Suppose Satan is trying to undermine a major Kingdom advance by sowing discord between leaders. Suddenly *(sniff, sniff)* they realize the real reason for the problems and together close the door on this black-and-white polecat.

Spiritual smell can be developed. Jesus had it, and that's what He demonstrated in the wilderness. And it works—"It" meaning a warning that the great skunk is around, so be careful. You and I can become adept at knowing when Stinky Satan is near! *(sniff, sniff)* "Whew! Awful. Let me out of here!"

What would you think if a skunk let loose his spray and someone you knew just stood around? What if that person said the smell wasn't so bad once you got used to it?

Would you respond, "Yes, I guess you're right"? Of course not!

But I fear too many Christians respond that way to the devil. You can tell by the conversations they join, the books they read, the movies they see, the music they hear, the way they're used by the enemy to keep others from Christ or to do damage to the Church. Satan's stench doesn't bother them anymore.

Am I referring to you?

I hope not!

*The Enchanter was wearing the robe of fire, a mastery of woven color: red and yellow patterns interwoven with orange and white and blue. Burners, each holding a glowing poker in their hands, climbed from the other cars. Soon the tall, proud man was surrounded by these guards.*

*The Enchanter ruled Enchanted City with fire. He loved fire, loved its power. He called it to himself and used it to cast spells. Long ago he had decreed night to be day and day to be night, because he was so jealous of the light of the sun.*

**From the *Tales of the Kingdom* story:**
**"The Enchanted City"**

# CHAPTER 3

# Prepare Ye the Way

～

KNOWING THAT SOMEONE important was to stay in your home
would mean, I presume, that you would make things as presentable as
possible. Should your guest be a president or a prime minister, you might
even do some quick redecorating, buy a new mattress for the guest room,
or whatever. But you would get ready!

So far we have looked at two aspects of the Kingdom: that the King is
the *christos*, the Messiah, the anointed one; and that we are in the midst of
a cosmic insurrection brought about by Satan—the clash of the kingdoms
of light and darkness. Now we are ready for a startling announcement:
The great King himself is coming to this world He created and still loves.
Get ready!

Who am I? "I am the voice of one crying in the wilderness, Prepare the
way of the Lord. Make his paths straight."

It is young John the Baptist speaking. You know how a modern highway
eliminates the curves and hills and dips for the convenience of travelers?
Well, in the same way John said we should get ready for God's great
anointed King. He was quoting Isaiah.

"Every valley shall be filled, and every mountain and hill shall be brought
low, and the crooked shall be made straight, and the rough ways shall be
made smooth, and all flesh shall see the salvation of God!"

It was an electrifying announcement. Remember that the Jews longed
for just such a prophetic word from God. "So great is this one who is to
come, that I'm not even worthy to carry his sandals for him," said John.

John's message was that the coming of God's anointed King merited
the special preparation of His subjects. Because the very Kingdom of God
was at hand, all should turn their lives around, repent, and drastically alter

the way they live. "Even now the axe is laid to the root of the trees; every tree therefore that does not bear good fruit is cut down and thrown into the fire."

"What should we do then?" asked the multitudes who followed John. He responded, in effect, "Live in a way that will be pleasing to your king! Soldiers—quit robbing people by violence or by false accusation, and be content with your wages. Tax collectors—collect no more than is appointed to you. He among you who has two coats, let him share with him who has none; and he who has food, let him do likewise. Why? This is the way your king would have it!"

Then one day something incredible happened. While baptizing converts, John saw the Messiah Himself enter the water and come toward him. After John had baptized this one of much higher rank than himself, the heavens suddenly opened, the Holy Spirit descended as a dove on the Christ, and a voice from heaven said, "Thou art my beloved Son"—a phrase from Psalm 2 that, interestingly enough, was sung at the coronation of Israel's kings. Then the voice added, "My beloved Son, with thee I am well pleased"—and from that moment on, I believe John knew that he must decrease and the Christ must increase.

*The coming of a great king warrants preparation.*

That was John's theme and the theme of this third chapter as well: *The coming of a great king warrants preparation.*

All this happened long ago, you may be thinking. But there is an added surprise. God's anointed King is coming again, a second time, and it's going to be even more spectacular than the first. The Christ Himself said, "As the lightning comes from the east and shines as far as the west [or as suddenly as the skies are lit up from one end to the other], so will be the next coming of the Son of Man with power and glory."

At this point, I believe the baptizer's warning about bearing good fruit bears repeating, because when the King comes next it will be as a judge: "Eyes like a flame of fire," wrote John the apostle, "On his head many diadems. Clad in a robe dipped in blood ... the armies of heaven follow him ... he will tread the wine press of the fury of the wrath of God."

The fact is, my friend, the time draws nearer and nearer. The period allowed for rebellion is coming to an end. This great occasion, marked by another opening of the heavens, means the next phase is here in the completion of the restoration. Even to talk about it, a preacher today, like his predecessor John, must quickly declare, "Don't make much over me; I'm not even worthy to shine this king's shoes!"

If this incredible event is possibly just over the horizon, a person would have to be a fool not to get ready. Prepare yourself! What you have heard about so many times, the hope we sing of in the church when we're together, is near—soon to be fulfilled. So start living now the way you want to be when your Monarch actually makes His appearance.

Perhaps you're thinking, *The message is clear and timely. But what can I do to get ready?*

That's a good question. For starters, turn away from anything that has even the slightest smell of the traitor, the evil one, the pretender. Walk the way you were intended to. Show the King the deference He deserves. Stop saying you don't have time to spend in His presence. Love the King even now with all your heart, soul, strength and mind, and show compassion toward others, especially those in need.

Not respecting God and being unconcerned for others is what ruined the initial paradise we were created to inhabit. What a phenomenal world this would be if everyone lived full of love for God and love for fellow human beings. How would you like to raise your family in that kind of a community? Why, the contrast to what we now know is beyond our wildest imaginations.

Someday, when the King returns to reign, I believe He will declare this lifestyle to be His expectation—that all men and women love Him with a full heart and act toward others the way they themselves would like to be treated. But it is also the lifestyle you should adopt right now, if you truly want to get ready for His return.

You can't do that all at once, however. Such a change involves so many areas of life that it has to be reduced to smaller chunks. Let me challenge you to work on just one dramatic alteration. I use the word "Dramatic" to emphasize the true significance of what you are doing—it is not merely a token.

Many years ago, my wife and I determined that we wanted to put all our efforts into the Kingdom. This meant a number of calculated choices, including getting rid of our television set. Among other considerations, it was eating up hours we felt could be spent more profitably in the cause of Christ.

Actually, this one simple decision profoundly affected how much we accomplish for the Kingdom—which is one way of measuring our love for Christ. It affected our prayer lives, our time in Scripture, our sense of holiness, and certainly our conscious awareness of the King's presence. It affected our relationships to one another and to our children; we now have more time for those in need, and more occasions to be with our brothers and sisters in Christ. That one simple, though dramatic, decision touched both the vertical and the horizontal planes of our lives, both the spiritual and the mundane.

But most of all, it helped us be more aware of our need to be ready for the King's return.

We're not opposed to television. In fact, we were both involved in the medium for many years in our work. All I'm trying to do is to give you an example, a living illustration of what I mean by "A dramatic move."

Like Zacchaeus, you may need to alter your attitude toward money. Like the apostles, perhaps you need to change your profession to demonstrate to your new King the seriousness of your intent. Or like Nicodemus, you may even have to put your reputation and position on the line. Not knowing your personal situation, I can't be more precise, but I do know that before most people expect it, a great trumpet blast will rend the heavens, and suddenly nothing in the world will matter, save one thing—*was I ready?*

At that time even your most dramatic changes in lifestyle will seem like tiny sacrifices indeed.

So how about it? Are you ready to take the first step?

"I baptize you with water for repentance, he will baptize you with fire." "Mine eyes have seen the glory of the coming of the Lord." "Make his paths straight." "He is trampling out the vintage where the grapes of wrath are stored." "The kingdom of heaven is at hand." "He has loosed the fateful lightnings of his terrible swift sword. His truth is marching on." "Glory, glory and Hallelujah!"

∿

*"They say that there's a stranger in the streets talking about another kingdom, and how foolish it is to live in the night, and that we all should follow him and not obey the Enchanter," said Theysay.*

*"**What?**" said both of his friends in amazement.*

*"**I** didn't say it," the third friend answered, shaking his head and backing away. "**They** said it."*

*The very next night, Triple Tongue noticed a stranger standing beneath his broadcast column. A soft light surrounded the man.*

**From the *Tales of the Resistance* story:**
**"Doubletalk, Triple Tongue and Theysay"**

CHAPTER 4

# BEST OF BOTH WORLDS

~

A LTHOUGH *KINGDOM* is a common-enough word, most people don't use it in everyday conversation. My guess is that it's one of those terms people think they know how to define—until they actually try to. Maybe you think of a kingdom as a place where a king rules instead of a president or a prime minister. But *kingdom* and *place* don't always go together. For instance, where can the animal kingdom, the plant kingdom, or the mineral kingdom be found on a map?

To understand the way the New Testament writers use the word *kingdom* (which, by the way, I believe is the most important term in all of the New Testament), it is necessary to realize that *kingdom* and *place* don't always go together.

Jesus talked all the time about His Kingdom, but never once did He imply that anyone could find it on a map. Spiritual kingdoms don't necessarily have geographic boundaries. When the Scriptures report, therefore, that Christ went through cities and villages preaching and bringing the good news of the Kingdom of God, He wasn't handing out Xeroxed sheets with directions as to how to get there.

What was He doing? Let me give you a simple answer.

Even though the Kingdom of God is one of the most profound truths in all of Scripture—volumes have been published on it and continue to be written—still, it is a paradoxically simple concept.

Our Lord was talking about any situation—and I'm deliberately using the word *situation*—in which (1) Christ is recognized as King, (2) His will is obeyed, and (3) obedient subjects reap the benefits of His reign. Heaven is the Kingdom of God because in that setting all three of these conditions are met.

When Christ returns to our planet and establishes His reign in Israel, as history is brought to a glorious close, the earth itself will know the Kingdom of God. That's because these same three elements will be present: Christ will be recognized as King, His word will be obeyed, and humanity will benefit immensely from His rule. Finally this bloody sphere will know peace. The Old Testament prophets say the land will produce so abundantly, the sower will have to hurry to get out of the way of the reaper who is right on his heels. Even in the animal kingdom the lion will stretch out next to the lamb.

But Jesus also preached to His hearers that for now, "The kingdom of God is in the midst of you."

How can this be?

Well, the requirements were fulfilled when any man or woman (1) bowed to him as King, (2) stated a commitment to live subservient to the King's wishes, and (3) was then snatched from Satan's domain by a supernatural act and began to immediately experience the benefits of life under the reign of Christ. When a group of such changed people come together, they demonstrate to the world what God intended society to look like.

Wherever those three elements are found, the Kingdom of God is present for everyone to see.

Viewing the Kingdom as the kingship, or the reign, of Christ explains why the terms *the kingdom of God* and *the kingdom of heaven* are used interchangeably in the gospels. They mean the same thing, much like *America* and *the United States*. For all practical purposes, they are synonymous.

An illustration of this is Matthew 19:23-24, in which Christ says it will be hard for a rich man to enter the "kingdom of heaven." Then He repeats, "Again I tell you, it is easier for a camel to go through the eye of a needle than for a rich man to enter the kingdom of God." So Christ Himself uses these terms interchangeably.

We find something similar in our Lord's prayer: "Thy kingdom come, thy will be done on earth as it is in heaven." In a sense, this is like the common device in Hebrew poetry whereby a thought is expressed and then repeated in the next line, though in different words. In 1 Chronicles 29, for example, David prays, "Thine is the kingdom, O Lord," and then in the next line he states the same idea with these words, "And thou art exalted as head above all."

Obviously, the New Testament book of Matthew was written in Greek, not Hebrew. Still, Christ's prayer has a Hebrew flavor when the idea of "Thy kingdom come" is repeated in the phrase "Thy will be done on earth as it is in heaven." In other words, "In heaven all see Christ as King, obey His will, and know great benefit as a result—may it be so here on earth as well. Thy Kingdom come!"

One great problem of our time is that too many who have supposedly bowed their knee to the King show little interest in obeying His will. And if such a basic commitment of Kingdom living is consistently violated, it is plain that one by one, the Kingdom benefits will begin to fall by the wayside.

If that doesn't make sense, assume for a moment the mindset of the King. Ask yourself how many favors you as a ruler would shower on subjects who verbally affirm you but in practice consistently copy the lifestyle of the kingdom of darkness.

It has been important to me to define those three elements that make up the Kingdom of God, or the kingdom of heaven, because you will find these two terms throughout the gospels. Here's a sample:

Matthew 7:21: "Not everyone who says to me, 'Lord, Lord,' shall enter the kingdom of heaven, but he who does the will of my Father who is in heaven."

Mark 12:34: "And when Jesus saw that he answered wisely, he said to him, 'You are not far from the kingdom of God.'"

Luke 17:20-21: "Being asked by the Pharisees when the kingdom of God was coming, he answered them, 'the kingdom of God is not coming with signs to be observed; nor will they say, "Lo, here it is!" or "There!" for behold, the kingdom of God is in the midst of you.'"

In John 18:33, 36-37, Pilate asked Jesus, "Are you the king of the Jews?" and Jesus said, "My kingdom is not of this world. If it were, my servants would fight to prevent my arrest by the Jews. But now my kingdom is from another place."

"You are a king, then!" said Pilate.

Jesus answered, "You are right in saying I am a king. In fact, for this reason I was born, and for this I came into the world, to testify to the truth."

Well, these passages are just a smattering of what you'll find in the gospels. The point is that the Kingdom is their dominant theme.

In the next chapter, you will discover how electrifying this Kingdom message sounds when preached by Christ. It will surprise you! And after that, I'll trace the Kingdom theme through the rest of the New Testament.

I've repeated it about as much as I dare, but I'll state one last time so no one could possibly miss it:

---

*Christ's Kingdom is any situation in which*
*(1) Christ is recognized as King, (2) His will is obeyed,*
*and (3) obedient subjects reap the benefit of His rule.*

---

～

*"Wait! Wait!" Hero exclaimed. "I don't understand. I don't understand anything."*

*Amanda stopped. Tendrils of hair were already loosened from her braid. Some of the wild flowers had fallen.*

*"What is a kingdom? The kingdom of what? Where is the Kingdom?"*

*Amanda's jaw dropped. She laughed in surprise. "Why, that's the first rule of Great Park: A Kingdom Is Anyplace Where the King Rules!"*

**From the *Tales of the Kingdom* story:**
**"The Faithless Ranger"**

# CHAPTER 5

# KINGDOM HYPE

~

I HAVE ALWAYS FELT that Jesus intended the beatitudes to be attention-getters rather than admonitions as to how people should live. These "blessings" (which is what beatitudes actually means) are found in Matthew 5 at the start of Christ's famous Sermon on the Mount. An abbreviated and slightly different form of these blessings is found in Luke 6. The beatitudes begin, "Blessed are the poor in spirit, for theirs is the kingdom of heaven. Blessed are those who mourn, for they will be comforted," and so on.

Now, what I mean by "Attention-getters" is that I don't believe Christ was saying His followers should become mourners in order to be comforted. Neither do I think He meant they should try to be poor in spirit, whatever that means, so that the Kingdom can be theirs. Incidentally, in Luke 6 the words "In spirit" aren't even included. So in that chapter, if the traditional approach is followed, the crowd would have heard Christ say that to be a part of His Kingdom, one is wise to be poor, or to at least act poor.

Even so, these verses are usually preached as instructions concerning the way we are to act. In other words, yes, we are to mourn, be poor in spirit, etc.

Granted, some of the beatitudes fit that framework. We should hunger and thirst for righteousness if we want to be satisfied (verse 6); we should be merciful if we wish to obtain mercy (verse 7); we should be pure in heart if we want to see God (verse 8). But again, in the context of Matthew's account of Christ's life and ministry, and especially in light of one special word used in the introduction to the sermon, I believe the beatitudes are an announcement, a proclamation, a marvelous attention-getting device. That one word is gospel, as it is used in Matthew 4:23: "He went about all Galilee teaching in their synagogues and preaching the gospel of the kingdom."

Now gospel, as you know, means "good news." Jesus went around preaching good news about the Kingdom of God. And I believe the beatitudes quickly highlight the good news He was talking about. That's why I like to paraphrase Christ's beatitudes this way: "Listen to me, people, I have good news for you. In what kingdom have the poor [or even the poor in spirit] been blessed? Never has this been the case! But in the kingdom I'm telling you about, because the poor are a personal concern of the king himself, they are truly blessed!"

Now that gets your attention, doesn't it?

Or try this: "Who listening to me right now lives in a kingdom where comfort is always offered to people who are mourning? No one! But again, you are truly blessed, for I'm telling you of a new kingdom where those who mourn are comforted! Sound good?"

"Are you who are meek and submissive always being imposed upon? Under my reign, people like you will not be taken advantage of. Rather, the most meek of you will inherit the earth."

You can almost hear the responsive rumble move through the ranks, can't you!

Christ continues: "Do you hunger and thirst for righteousness? Then follow me and you'll find it! Be merciful and be blessed. For when I reign as your rightful sovereign, the merciful will in turn discover mercy. In fact, for those who are pure in heart, I tell you the pure in heart shall see God. What greater blessing can anyone want? And I promise to provide it! And peacemakers, your blessing will be that you will be called 'sons of God.'"

Can't you just feel the electricity in a crowd that hears these words?

"Now do any of you know what persecution is?" Jesus was all too familiar with the conditions under which these people lived. "You know persecution only too well, but here's more good news. If your persecution is for the sake of righteousness, my special kingdom will be yours forever. So you see, even when men revile you and persecute you and utter all kinds of evil against you falsely on my account, you can rejoice and be glad. For your reward is great in heaven, for so men persecuted the prophets who were before you."

Now if this isn't a good way to capture a crowd, I don't know what is. Think of the Jews under Roman rule as being much like the Poles once were under Soviet domination. You can imagine the stir if a dynamic young Polish leader came along and declared, "I offer you an alternative rule."

The response would be overwhelming. As Matthew reports, "Great crowds followed him from Galilee and the Decapolis and Jerusalem and Judea and from beyond Jordan."

Again, how to interpret Christ's words is a matter of opinion. Perhaps Matthew does mean that Jesus was saying, "Be glad that you're poor. Being poor is a blessing in disguise. Don't you know that the poor are much more likely to get to heaven? So you're fortunate if you're poor!" But still, I think it would be hard to excite a crowd that way. And who would want to come back for the next message?

I can't imagine Christ was actually saying, "It's not hard to be meek, friends. Try it, you'll like it! You have the earth and its beauty and its great ability to produce. Be happy with that. Don't envy those who supposedly experience the good life. It's not all it's cracked up to be."

Would people still be listening to Jesus two thousand years later if that's all He was saying? Wouldn't a heckler have yelled, "Forget it, pal—come on Reuben, let's go home!"

Perhaps Jesus intended His words to be heard the way they're traditionally taught—as instructions for life. But back in the original setting, I really don't see crowds rallying behind such a message, do you?

I fear that in our society, we are so used to overstatement, hype and intense competition for the eyes and ears of the public—a false kind of attention-getting—that we are apt to miss the most electrifying message to the common man this world has ever known: Christ's public introduction of the Kingdom of God.

Isn't it true today that the world's little people should be thrilled anew by Christ's good news about the kingdom? Allow me to restate that as my key sentence for this chapter:

*The world's little people should be thrilled anew
by Christ's good news of the Kingdom.*

Maybe this message doesn't interest the wealthy, the powerful or the famous, because often they are busy looking for more wealth, power and fame. That is why Jesus said it was so hard for them to enter the kingdom of which He spoke.

But for common folk like us—who knows an option that compares to this one? Bow before Christ as your king, submit to His rule, and reap the benefits of His reign—that's what becoming a part of the Kingdom involves.

You who are poor in spirit—in His Kingdom you won't remain second-class! Slave, child, female, Gentile—for everyone alike, this ruler will become your brother! You who mourn—this king cares when you hurt.

Where else can you find a government head who even knows your name, much less shows personal concern for you? Hear me! King Jesus specializes in healing broken hearts.

Are you feeling lowly, are you meek? At the restoration you will inherit the earth. Do you hunger and thirst for righteousness, for what is fair and just? Then you will have what you're seeking in Christ's Kingdom—and, let me quickly add, nowhere else.

Do you see what you're being offered? Does it excite you, or is it all old-hat? Put yourself in the context of those who first heard our Lord preach and you can begin, perhaps, to sense their excitement. Even in a free country where most people enjoy the daily benefits of affluence, I can't help but feel that many people will be gripped by Christ's proclamation. And He gave all He promised. It wasn't campaign rhetoric; it was—and still is—the truth of the universe.

Let me encourage you to respond to Christ's promises. Simply offer Him a prayer of gratitude, a prayer that expresses your thanks to the King for the grand opportunity you have of being part of His Kingdom.

Maybe you have never expressed such a thought before. Or perhaps you feel this kind of gratitude every day. In either case, simply pray something like the following: "Jesus, the Kingdom thrills me. And yes, I'm glad your reign includes heaven. But that it's also here and now—how wonderful! We have the best of both worlds! May the reality of your Kingdom be an increasingly vital part of my consciousness. Thy kingdom come, thy will be done on earth as it is in heaven. Yes!"

A simple prayer of thanks for the privilege of full citizenship in the greatest kingdom of all time is not only appropriate, but it also seals in the subject's heart the importance of this relationship. Right now, take just a moment to voice, perhaps even write down, your own words of gratitude for this wonderful kingdom offered to us by Christ.

～

*And Thespia became a street player in the back alleys and dead-ends of Enchanted City, acting out the King's story in such a way that all who saw her suspected—then hoped—that there was a real Kingdom. Like the King, she worked in common clothes, and she never gave the luxuries of the Palace a backward glance, because when one has found one's real love it is easy to leave what has only been pretend.*

**From the *Tales of the Resistance* story:
"The Most Beautiful Player of All"**

# CHAPTER 6

# TOPICAL STUDY

❧

*Dear David Mains,*

*For twelve years I was affiliated with a denomination that was always talking about "kingdom work." No Gospel was preached, but they were as busy as bees, trying to bring in this kingdom. Frankly I see no place in the Bible where Jesus is called king of the church. So Brother Mains, I know you love the Lord, and you can go on trying to build the kingdom. But I say when you're all done there's not going to be anyone in it!*

THIS LETTER came from a listener of my *Chapel of the Air* radio broadcasts. Despite her disagreement with me, I think I understand where this woman is coming from. Given her background of exposure to liberal theology and its version of a Kingdom emphasis, I might have reacted the same way.

Here is the crux of the misunderstanding: Christ's Kingdom will never be complete before His return. Believers won't transform this earth into anything remotely resembling heaven before the great King's Second Coming. I am not advocating that Christians attempt to bring in the Kingdom by themselves, although such a challenge has been falsely preached from many pulpits.

No, Christians cannot usher in Christ's Kingdom. But they should be involved in advancing it.

I wrote back to this woman, "Though I know you love the Lord, you're mistaken. Jesus is king over His people, even as He is the head of His Body, the Church. I think you know that, but you just don't feel it the way I believe you should."

Let me illustrate. Several decades back, my second son Joel became very interested in the royal wedding of Prince Charles and Lady Diana. Joel was in his first year of junior high at the time. Knowing it would please him, his Aunt Fran gave Joel a beautiful large book with many full-color photographs of the royal couple. He was thrilled.

One of Joel's friends, Charlie, came by and looked all through his book. Joel asked if he too was interested in this prince and his bride-to-be.

"Prince, what Prince?" Charlie asked.

"Prince Charles," Joel responded, "The next in line to the throne of England. The guy you've been looking at in the book."

"You mean this man in the picture here?" questioned Charlie.

"Of course," was Joel's incredulous reply. "Who did you think he was?"

"Well, how was I supposed to know he's a prince? Here he's playing polo, and in this picture he's fishing. Here he's got on one of those Scottish kilts—and on this page he's in a carriage!"

"Come on, Charlie," said Joel, "Where have you been? You can't be that dumb. Of course he's a prince!"

Sound unreal? It is. I made up that conversation. But a lot of people look repeatedly at God's book and still don't perceive that there are scores of pictures in it of Christ as the greatest king this world has ever known. They see Jesus in His various roles—healer, teacher, and so on—but they entirely miss His major role as king. Jesus Himself emphasized His kingship. Yet somehow this great truth has not clicked into place for many people—even many believers.

Perhaps you think the Kingdom is emphasized in the gospels, but not in Acts or the epistles. Let me suggest that you do a topical Bible study—in this case, specifically looking through the New Testament for the idea of the Kingdom of God, or the kingdom of heaven.

Begin by compiling a list of all the times those phrases appear. Using a concordance, write down each reference and what it says. For instance: Acts 8:12—Philip preached in Samaria about the Kingdom of God.

Surprisingly, you'll end up with over two pages of verses containing New Testament references to the Kingdom other than those that appear in the gospels. And that's just a start.

Next, pursue related words to further develop the topic. Some will be obvious, like king. Certain king references in the concordance will have no value to this study. For instance, in Acts the listings referring to King

Herod and King Agrippa will not pertain to the kingdom of heaven. But in Acts 17:7, the people at Thessalonica accuse the Christians of acting against Caesar by saying there is another king—Jesus. This is a helpful reference that should be written down.

Tracing other related words, like *ruler, crown, throne, scepter, sovereign, reign* and *glory*, reveal even more aspects of the Kingdom.

A third and final step is to note Kingdom-type references as you read through Scripture in your daily Bible time. Any thoughts or words that have a bearing on the topic might yield information otherwise overlooked. Let me give you an example from my own study. 2 Peter 1:11 caught my interest because Peter writes, "There will be provided for you an entrance into the eternal kingdom of our Lord and Savior Jesus Christ." Checking my master sheet, I saw I had recorded that reference already. But at verse 16 I hit pay dirt. Here was a strong word I hadn't found before—and how descriptive: "For we did not follow cleverly devised myths," writes Peter, "When we made known to you the power and coming of our Lord Jesus Christ, but we were eyewitnesses of his majesty." The phrase almost jumped off the page when I read it—his majesty.

I remember one time asking myself: *How would I address a real king?* I decided I would probably call him "Your majesty." But would I be comfortable saying that to God? After reading the passage from Peter, I had to bow my head, greatly moved, and say thanks. He had taught me the grandeur and appropriateness of these words—His majesty.

Can I still say "Father" when I pray? Of course. But I learned that other terms are appropriate too.

The fact is, the truth of Christ's kingship is sprinkled all through Acts, the Epistles, and Revelation. Consider such well-known phrases as these: Every knee shall bow; Christ is seated at the right hand of God; all things are under his feet; God hath highly exalted him, above all rule and authority and power and dominion; made worthy of the kingdom of God; heirs of the kingdom which he promised; a kingdom that cannot be shaken; by his appearing and his kingdom; flesh and blood cannot inherit the kingdom of God; fellow members of the kingdom of God; transferred us to the kingdom of his beloved Son; I, John, your brother who shares with you in Jesus the tribulation and the kingdom…

And that is just a sampling of the riches of Kingdom imagery the Bible has to share. And none of these phrases are from the gospels.

Some Christians may be like rebellious Anna in the play The King and I. When she sees the Siamese ruler lording it over people, she sings, "Yes, your majesty, no, your majesty—show me how low to bow, your majesty..." But her sarcasm doesn't alter the fact that the king is still the king. And in the same way:

*We do well to be reminded of the majesty of Christ.*

In terms of being raised in the church, I'm not much different than the woman whose letter appears at the beginning of this chapter. Yet in all those years right up through high school, the Kingdom somehow escaped me. I don't think it was ever mentioned.

Then I studied at Wheaton College, where the school motto is: *For Christ and His Kingdom.* Even more importantly, as a student under the ministry of Dr. V. Raymond Edman, the president of Wheaton College, I came to have a new appreciation of the Kingdom.

Dr. Edman died while preaching a college chapel service. Although I had graduated by that time, I know the story well. He was talking about the proper way to come into the presence of a great king. His illustration was of a time he had an audience with Haile Selassie (then the ruler of Ethiopia), and Dr. Edman detailed the preparation that was necessary.

Then his message shifted as he talked about believers coming into the presence of a much greater king. He spoke of how we need to be clothed in the robes of righteousness. While he talked—in the middle of that sentence—he was gone. From Wheaton College Chapel he was issued into the courts of the King of the Universe about whom he spoke. How fitting! I have no doubt that he was ready.

Just as Dr. Edman helped me understand the Kingdom, maybe I can help others as well. That would please me. As in college days, when assignments sometimes covered several months of work, why not consider doing a topical Bible study concerning the Kingdom as a "semester project."

I can't predict how it will affect your grade, but knowing more about the Kingdom should prepare you well for the final!

The Fire Wizard stomped in rage on the pavement. "Who do you think you are? Insurrector! Rebel! Miscreant!" His voice rose in a crescendo of fury.

Hero crept closer, despite the danger. He wanted to see the man in the middle who was hidden by the crowd.

A calm voice answered. "I am the King. I am the true ruler of this city. The time for the restoration of my Kingdom is at hand."

**From the *Tales of the Resistance* story:**
**"The Challenger"**

CHAPTER 7

# POINT OF ENTRY

~

I SUSPECT SOME PEOPLE reading this book aren't sure whether or not they belong to Christ's wonderful Kingdom. This chapter is for them. Even if you have gone to church for many years, you might still experience some long-standing confusion on this matter. Perhaps it's painful to admit you're insecure as to whether Jesus, God's anointed King, has confirmed that you really belong to His Kingdom.

If we were talking face-to-face, you might say, "David, I understand about not being able to point to Christ's Kingdom on a map. That makes sense. But it still confuses me as to who is in the Kingdom and who isn't. At least in men's kingdoms the roads are marked so you know when you get there!"

Simply stated: How do you find your way to Christ's Kingdom? And how do you know when you have made entry?

Let me put things into perspective by asking five key questions.

*1.   If Christ were to welcome you into His Kingdom today, how would this affect the way you presently live? What changes would being a subject of the King make in your life?*

*2.   Jesus Himself said it was wise for a person to count the cost of any decision. He told about a man who put up a tower and only half-finished the job. Everyone laughed at him because he hadn't carefully thought through the project before jumping into it. The point is that people contemplating Kingdom involvement should seriously consider what it will be like living under royal law.*

That last phrase, royal law, comes from James, the half-brother of Jesus, who writes in James 2:8, "If you really fulfill the royal law [that is, the law of the king], you shall love your neighbor as yourself." The other half of the royal law (or "great commandment," as Christ expressed it in Matthew 22) is, "You should love the Lord with all your heart and with all your soul, and with all your mind."

Now that's a big change for most of us. So are you ready to (1) show God the love He deserves and (2) demonstrate real concern for others? Well, that's a basic requirement in the Kingdom. It was both taught and modeled by the Monarch Himself, and it's expected behavior for all the King's subjects. Think it through. If you don't want to show love for God and love for people, you probably shouldn't consider becoming one of this King's followers.

*3.    Have you fallen short of this standard? Do you miss the stated target: love for God and love for fellow human beings?*

If so, then you understand what Scripture calls "sin," which simply means "To miss the mark." If this sounds too simplistic, consider what a phenomenal change would occur in society if everyone hit the mark! Can you imagine what it would be like in your community if everyone consistently loved God and other people?

Refusing to give God the love He deserves, and putting oneself ahead of others, is at the very center of the curse man experienced in the Garden of Eden that made living so difficult. And do you realize that when you "miss the mark," you personally contribute to the problems this world knows?

*4.    Do you think you can bring about these necessary changes through self-effort? Are you capable of loving God and others by mere self-determination? Can you pull it off without divine help?*

The answer to those questions is obviously no. Even if you could love both God and people for a while, how would you deal with the problem of your past offenses? And if past sin isn't forgiven, you will never experience what Paul writes about in Colossians 1:13: "... being delivered from the dominion of darkness and transferred to the kingdom of God's beloved son."

But further in that chapter you'll discover that in spite of our estrangement from God (Colossians 1:21-22), "hostile in mind, doing evil deeds … Christ has reconciled us to God." In other words, He has made us friends with God again "In Christ's body of flesh by his death." Do you believe that?

5.    *Do you believe Christ is able to supernaturally change who you are? Can Christ, through His death and resurrection, infuse your life with power to walk in a new and better way? Do you think Christ can hear your request and, by an act of His mercy, forgive you and grant you this great favor?*

If you believe Christ can do that—even though you can't prove it— there is within you the beginning of what the Bible calls "faith." If your heart whispers, "Yes, I believe Jesus can do that," then you are very close to his kingdom. This is exactly the kind of faith a person needs to enter in.

6.    *If you feel Christ can change you, when would be a good time to ask Him to do this?*

If you answered "now," I suggest you bow immediately before this King. Literally bowing is the best, perhaps alone in your room. If that isn't possible, at least mentally go down on one knee and picture yourself as a subject before your sovereign. From that kneeling position, tell the King you want to change, that you want to live in the way that will please Him as your monarch. You want His Spirit, the King's Spirit, to enter you, to cleanse you of all past disobedience, all your offenses against Him and your sins against others. Tell Him you desire His Spirit to make your body His home and that you want Him to begin the process of tutoring you in the royal law of His Kingdom.

Just one more thing—while you are bowing, imagine that you are at the foot of a cross. Why? Because:

---

*Bowing before the great King's cross is a good way to enter Christ's Kingdom.*

---

Do you have that picture in mind? As you kneel, realize your Lord is on the cross because of you, because you have fallen short of His glory, because you consistently missed the mark.

Now listen to the thief who agonizes on the cross next to Christ's. Overhear him say to the third dying man, "Do you not fear God? We are receiving the due reward of our deeds, but this man has done nothing wrong. Jesus, remember me, when you come into your kingdom!"

As you picture this scene and hear the thief make his plea, quickly add, "Me too, Jesus. I want the same thing. I feel the way that man does. Can you hear me praying too?"

In this greatest drama of all history—now playing itself out on your personal behalf—with darkness and the earth trembling and bystanders weeping, I believe you will hear the King's answer in your heart. Jesus, above whose head are the words "This is the King of the Jews," will silently whisper to your soul, "Truly, I say to you, you also will be with me in paradise!"

Hundreds of times in my life I've brought people to this sacred place where I first came to know Him. Never once have I been with someone who heard Jesus say no. Recently I spoke with a young woman in her late twenties. She was weary and marred in many ways by the world, its sin, and her participation in it.

She asked me, "What if Jesus says no? Or worse, suppose He refuses to answer me? So many have treated me that way. If Jesus does, I fear it'll be the final insult I could take."

"I feel your fear," I told her. "But I've known this King a long time, and never once have I seen Him act that way toward anyone. It would be inconsistent with what I know about Him."

And I was right! In a matter of minutes, after she made her request at the cross, she was saying, "Thank you, Jesus, thank you so much for hearing me."

And I see this prayer of gratitude being yours as well when you request deliverance from the dominion of darkness and when you ask to be welcomed into the Kingdom of God's beloved Son.

John, a disciple and beloved friend of the Lord, wrote in the first chapter of his gospel, "To all who received him, who believed in his name, he gave power to become children of God, who were born not of blood nor of the will of man, but of God." Two chapters later in his gospel, John uses a similar expression—being born anew—as a way of entering the Kingdom of God.

For you, if you are concerned about your status in the Kingdom, going to the cross and experiencing this new birth might be the most important item on your immediate agenda. Enter the gates now. It's the only point of entry to the Kingdom of God, and you wouldn't want to miss it!

~

*The warm flood had reached her toes. Dirty felt as if she were being held by the King, just like the Crippled Girl. She felt his kiss. Mercie was right—you did not have to see the King to be surrounded by the power of his love.*

*Dirty heard music. The violinists and the harpists had begun to play. It was time for the dance, which began the celebrations. She had watched it many times from the outside. Now she was in the middle. All the subjects joined hands in one huge circle.*

*Dirty wanted to dance. She wanted to sing and shout. She turned to Mercie. "The King **does** love me! I'm clean! I'm clean! The King has made me clean!"*

**From the *Tales of the Kingdom* story:**
**"The Girl Named Dirty"**

CHAPTER 8

# PEOPLE OF SIGNIFICANCE

~

W HAT DO YOU THINK the possibilities are that the world will take a significant turn for the better? Do you have such a hope, or do you feel the problems are so many that there's really no cause for optimism?

Or approach it from a different angle. Suppose a major breakthrough could actually come about. What would be the key? Politics? Economics? Diplomacy? Weaponry?

How would you respond to a man in his early thirties who insists that, if we are to improve the world, the most important area of all is the spiritual? I ask because that's what Christ advocated in His message about the Kingdom of God. There is no denying it; from the start Jesus intended His mission to affect the entire earth for good. Not that He predicted the world would change overnight, of course, or even that great numbers of people would become part of His Kingdom. But He believed His servants would profoundly affect society. They would play a strategic role in improving the well-being of the entire world.

How? One needs hardly to argue the point. Imagine an ever-increasing number of people who, because they bow to the King and obey His will, give food to the hungry; clothe the naked; welcome the stranger; visit the sick; go to those in prison; forgive seventy times seven times; love their neighbor as themselves and likewise their enemy; whose word is as good as an oath; who being forced to go one mile, will go two; who won't commit adultery even in their minds; who are not anxious about material possessions; who don't judge others; who work for justice; who pray for good; who live as servants; who, with hearts of love, are agents of reconciliation; and on whose lips is the good news of God's forgiveness. Well, such people will influence their world profoundly!

You see, Christ never expected sinful people to maintain a high moral standard. He asked quite realistically, "Can a bad tree bear good fruit?" But with His Kingdom, He offered hope. In it, forgiveness for sin was available from God Himself. The lifestyle most beneficial to all was clearly spelled out—love for the Lord and love for one's neighbor. On top of that, power to enflesh this ideal was available through the Holy Spirit, so Kingdom members were to set a whole new standard.

The truth is that the fate of the world's goodness literally hinges on the success of the Kingdom. Its members are extremely important because they are society's real hope. And that's not my idea—it's Christ's.

Jesus often made this clear. "You are the leaven," he said, "That causes the whole of the loaf to rise." "You are the salt of the earth"; that is, Kingdom members are the preserving element that keeps the world from going bad. They add that "Extra" flavoring that makes life palatable. He said, "The eye is what lets light into the body. If the eye is bad, the whole body is in darkness." Kingdom people are the eye of the body of mankind. "You are the city on the hill," He said, meaning we fill a strategic position and cannot help but be seen. He also said, "You are the light of the world. You illuminate the darkness for the benefit of everyone else."

In other words, He was saying this:

*Kingdom members must understand that mankind's hope for a better world rests upon them.*

In our time, the servants of the King can significantly affect their world, whether or not they get written up in Time or Newsweek. Whether the Jerusalem Courier or the Galilee Free Press (to invent some examples) got a picture story out of what Jesus' Kingdom members were doing in His day was not significant; news coverage never determines the true importance of events. Still, the King's servants must realize that, from God's perspective, mankind's hope rests with them.

Now it's one thing to hear such a challenge expressed today, but imagine how it must have felt to be in that crowd that first heard such words from the lips of Jesus. Just a few people, He says, could change the entire Roman world! "To what shall I compare the kingdom of God?" He asks. "It is like leaven which a woman took and hid in three measures of meal till it was all leavened."

You can almost hear the crowd stirring. Skeptical looks are seen on every side.

"You're going to need a shipload of leaven then, Mr. Nazarene," someone in the crowd might respond. "You don't know Rome. They glut on blood. Go to their arenas. It's butchery, pure and simple. The fighters have nothing to protect themselves. Their bodies are open to every blow. Kill, flog, bum. Why boggle at the slaughter? They use the lash to force them on to the sword."

Someone else adds, "We're fighting Rome, mister. R-O-M-E, where war is training men, moving men, marching men—fighting, stabbing, spearing, crushing, obliterating—no mercy. That's Rome."

"Visit their glorious city," another heckler continues. "See the luxury of the few and tell them to love their neighbor. Get the emperor to walk through the fetid slums and talk to the landlords who squeeze out every penny. Political intrigue, crime, murder in the streets—don't go out at night, Jesus!"

The skepticism is growing now. Another person yells, "Tell the Romans how you're going to feed the poor. Share your ideas at one of their banquets. Weird tastes, exotic rarities—anything bizarre to feed the world's rulers. Pies made out of parrots' tongues are great for the nobility. But if it's for the emperor, all those birds had to know how to talk before they were baked. Slavery, homosexuality, rape, hate, greed—how much leaven do you think you're going to need to lift that loaf, Jesus?"

Another challenge comes: "Look, just go to Golgotha outside Jerusalem. Watch what Romans do to world-changers. They strip them naked, stretch out their arms and legs, pound nails into their hands, jam a spike in their feet, and hang them up in the sun to scream and sweat and die!"

Calmly, firmly, Jesus asserts, "You are the salt of the earth."

"It's always been this way," someone complains. "I think we could empty out the entire salt shaker and it wouldn't make any difference. You know what I mean? There needs to be more of a program, sir. This idea of a spirit giving leadership is much too nebulous. And ease up on the thunder words. You're offending the religious leaders, threatening their positions. We'll never make it without our religious establishment."

"You are the eye that lets light into the entire body," says Jesus.

"Ha, ha. We may be the eye, young man. But this ain't the day the world's gonna listen to no Jews!"

"I'm just a bit overwhelmed, Master. You see, I'm only a little farmer who…"

"I'm studying to be a merchant, but, Jesus, my wife and I are just getting a home established."

"Sure, I have some money, Rabbi, but at the moment cash is hard to come by and…"

"You are the city on the hill that will be seen," Jesus says.

"Hey, does He realize how big this world is and how many people there are in it, to say nothing of the number of languages? And if you quiz them all, most will never even have heard of Palestine. If we're on a hill, they're on mountains!"

"You don't light a lamp to put it under a bushel, but on a lampstand," the Master continues, unperturbed. "You are the light of the world."

"Rabbi, if God wants to save this world, He will. And nothing you do or say will change it."

What would you say if you were there? How would you respond to this strange king's thoughts about the possibility of his kingdom affecting the entire world for good?

It is exciting to realize that many of Christ's original listeners not only believed that Jesus was the light of the world, but that they, as His followers, were lights as well. They understood that mankind's hope for something better rested chiefly on them, that the message of the Kingdom encompassed something more than just their personal conversions. Thank God for those early Christians and for their faith—because in the middle of an absolutely vile period of human history, they went out and turned the world upside down.

Can the same be said of Kingdom members today? Or have the majority of us decided to remove our mantle of significance? Have we joined others in a hopeless search for a better world in areas where the One who fashioned it is not allowed to play His role as sovereign? May this never be! Inhabitants of the Kingdom must understand that the hope for a better world rests with them—and nowhere else.

If this chapter accomplishes nothing more than helping you understand the significance of that statement above, I will be satisfied. As Christians, we do not have the privilege of looking elsewhere for solutions. If the world is to know a better day, Christians must look anew at the contribution our King expects us to make.

If that's our worldview, we will follow Christ and press the battle against the true enemy of God and man—"The ancient foe, who seeks to work us woe." Or to use Martin Luther's words:

> And though this world with devils filled
> Should threaten to undo us,
> We will not fear, for God hath willed
> His truth to triumph through us.
>
> Then let goods and kindred go,
> This mortal life also;
> The body they may kill:
> God's truth abideth still,
> His kingdom is forever!

~

*Hero's heart swelled with this honor. He would be a Ranger. He would fight for the King. He would give his forever pledge to protect the Kingdom, to be faithful. "To the King!" he shouted.*

*"To the King!" all shouted back.*

*"To the Restoration!"*

*With that, Commander turned to Hero and offered his hand. "Welcome, Ranger. The world goes not well, but the Kingdom comes."*

**From the *Tales of the Resistance* story:
"Back to Enchanted City"**

CHAPTER 9

# Better Days Ahead

~

SOMETIMES NEWSPAPER REPORTERS stop people on the street and ask the question: "In your opinion, what would be a good sign of better days ahead?"

You can imagine the variety of answers one might hear: "For me it would be the signing of a nuclear-arms limitation treaty." Or, "When some clever diplomat finds a permanent solution to the Palestinian problem." Or perhaps, "A woman president would bring peace."

My response might seem a little strange in a newspaper. I would reply, "Better days are ahead when Christians again take seriously the way Christ said His followers were to live!" That might surprise the average reporter! But I believe my answer represents Christ's own thinking. In the last chapter, I explained how Christ made it quite clear that mankind's hope for a better world rested squarely on the shoulders of the members of His Kingdom.

Don't get me wrong. I'm not implying, of course, that by mere diligence in our commitment to Christ we can usher in the Kingdom of God, as some have taught. Not for a minute! Never will we experience the Kingdom in its complete form throughout the world until the King Himself returns. But this doesn't mean believers should put off living by Kingdom standards until that time.

In the early Church, the Kingdom lifestyle was enfleshed immediately by its participants. Let me illustrate. First of all, the early Church believed that when Christ returned to reign, people would see the world's goods being shared among all people, maybe not equally, but certainly more fairly. So Kingdom members began working at such a practice. Since serving one another would be exemplified during the future reign of their King—

or so the early Christians reasoned—why wait? Let's be servants of one another right now!

Won't the future be free of worry because of Christ's very presence? So let's stop being anxious right this moment. Won't justice and compassion go hand-in-hand with law and order? Then why delay, they asked; why not practice justice and compassion even now?

Since the world under Christ's reign of peace will put aside war as a means of settling differences, many early believers refused to get sucked into the military affairs of the Romans. Would men respect God's gift of the earth itself? So they would demonstrate now their appreciation of God's good earth and certainly obey His laws about fields and resources. Slavery, exploitation, dehumanization—all would be taboo in Christ's coming Kingdom. Many early believers, therefore, eliminated these things from their lives as well.

As people living in submission to God's present and future King, Christ, these Christians became models of remade humanity. Corporately as an ever-growing Church, they demonstrated before their world how society would look when clothed in the garments of God. Reduced to its essentials, the Kingdom lifestyle involved loving God with all their heart, soul, mind and strength, and loving their neighbors as themselves. This standard, they knew, had come from the Monarch Himself—Jesus Christ.

Of course, at first these early students or disciples found it tremendously difficult to live the Kingdom way. But in time they became proficient at it. Thus the Kingdom of God became highly visible in those centuries. Its presence made a powerful difference in the world, just as Christ had said it would.

The point is this:

*The possibility of societal renaissance is initiated as the King's subjects commit themselves to the Kingdom lifestyle.*

By renaissance, I mean a reshaping or refashioning of the ways of the world—a regenesis, if you please, a new beginning. You see, this world's hope for a better future rests on believers adopting the Kingdom lifestyle.

The world is changed by individuals allowing the Spirit of Christ to initiate change in their own lives.

There had to be a noticeable difference between the way of the world and the lifestyle of the Kingdom. As the song from Godspell put it, "The tallest candlestick ain't much good without a wick. You got to live right to be the light of the world." Or in the words of our great King Himself: "If the salt has lost its savor, wherewith will the earth be salted?"

This is why I would tell the reporter that I believe you can forecast a better day for the world when Christians again take seriously the way Christ said His followers were to live. In the years after Christ's ascension, believers did just that—they lived the way Christ instructed them to. And the influence of Christianity was incredible!

What about now? As in the New Testament times, to be a Kingdom participant and not live by Kingdom standards is still unthinkable. Why? Because as Christians, we are to model for our generation humanity as it was originally intended by God: loving Him and loving others.

Corporately, the Church should still demonstrate before the public the appearance of God's new society. Although the Church is only a small percentage of the population, it is significant beyond its numbers because it reflects the Maker's design for interpersonal relationships throughout the world. "Looking for God's love?" the Church asks. "Then we'll model it for you! Justice? Step this way! Concern for the poor and the powerless? It's right before your very eyes as we live it out!"

Today we are still a part of the King's ongoing witness in history. Christ's challenge is still: "Let your light so shine before men that they may see your good works and give glory to your Father who is in heaven."

A story might be appropriate here. Before the time of electric railroad-crossing gates, an old fellow was in charge of one particular crossing. Sitting in his little cabin at night, dozing in and out of consciousness, he would sometimes hear the rattle of the tracks in the distance. He would then quickly grab his lantern from the wall and run out into the night to warn any cars that a train was coming.

But one time he had waited a little too long. Headlights were already coming up the road, and the train was fast approaching. Hurriedly he ran down the highway, swinging the lantern in a wide arc back and forth, screaming, "Stop! Stop!"

At the last minute, he jumped out of the way of the car as it raced past him and smashed into the freight.

When the authorities put the old fellow on trial for negligence, his astute railroad lawyers proved beyond doubt that the young people in the car had been drinking and that the old gentleman was respected in the community and considered trustworthy. He would probably have gotten off, but the prosecuting lawyer happened to ask: "In your hurry, old-timer, did you think to light the lantern?"

Is this not our fatal flaw as well? Christians have inundated the world with words, but does the world really see the contrast between their system and Christ's in action, between the lifestyle of the world and the lifestyle of the Kingdom? Like ancient Israel, do we reflect too much of the pagan culture that surrounds us? If our lantern has not been lit, then tragedy is near.

With all my heart I believe a societal renaissance would come about if the great King's subjects committed themselves to the Kingdom lifestyle. People would see the lantern of our testimony even before they heard our words.

In several places in Scripture the Kingdom lifestyle is spelled out. In Christ's Sermon on the Mount (Matthew 5-7), for instance. Read through it carefully, not as a way to enter the Kingdom, but for the purpose of understanding the Kingdom lifestyle. Study each item and ask yourself: "Is this true of me or not? Do I commit adultery in my mind? Do I judge others? Is clothing a fetish to me? Am I anxious about food and shelter? Do I forgive others when they wrong me?"

Such honest self-examination will help you decide how well you are living up to the King's decrees—the decrees by which all of us will someday live under his reign. Believers should be characterized by that kind of lifestyle right now; they choose by faith to participate in the Kingdom even before their King's return.

Of course, the exciting part is that our King is not asking us to live any differently than the way He lived Himself. So if this challenge sounds difficult, remember that it is also Christlike. With His help, we can learn to adopt the lifestyle of the Kingdom and become more like Jesus Himself.

And as we do, it will be a great sign that better days are ahead.

*Big Operator smiled, but it was a grim expression. He put his arm around the lad's shoulders. "Make no mistake. The Enchanter is evil and he's dangerous—never forget it. The closer the Restoration, the more Sightings of the King—the more dangerous and desperate he will become." Then his smile became almost cocky. "But the truth is, the Enchanter only has power over those who fear him. Here in the Taxi Resistance, we are subjects of the King. Consequently, we are not afraid."*

**From the *Tales of the Resistance* story:
"The Taxi Resistance"**

# CHAPTER 10

# A STYLE WORTHY OF THE KING

∿

WEARING NEW CLOTHES makes you feel good—especially if somebody notices!

For many years I picked out all my own clothes, but no one ever said, "Hey, David, you really look sharp!" So when my wife, Karen, bought me a suit once, I stuck up my nose at it. It just wasn't my style, I thought. But I wore it and wouldn't you know—that very day, three or four people told me how good I looked. Never had that happened before—ever! Now I always ask Karen to go with me when I shop for new clothes.

Well, in this chapter I want you to consider trying on a new spiritual outfit, this time chosen with the help of another person, namely, the Apostle Paul.

No, I'm not digressing from our Kingdom theme. I'm emphasizing that Paul, who certainly had a Kingdom mindset, often wrote about how we should live "In a manner worthy of the Lord," in a manner appropriate for one who serves God's anointed King.

To live in a manner worthy of the Lord is Paul's stated desire in a number of his letters. I expressed a similar thought in the last chapter; the subjects of the great King should commit themselves to the kingdom lifestyle. Paul's point is the same, only he uses a vivid word-picture to express it.

For example, in Colossians 3 he writes that to be worthy of this exalted one who is seated at the right hand of God, who will be appearing again in glory, we must remove—like a garment—that which formerly characterized us, and in its place we must put on spiritual clothing befitting our king. The following four verses (Colossians 3:9, 10, 12 and 13, with my emphases added) give you a good idea of Paul's general picture:

Do not lie to one another, seeing that you have put off the old nature with its practices and have put on the new nature. Put on then as God's chosen ones, compassion, kindness, lowliness, meekness, and patience. And if one has a complaint against another, forgiving each other; as the Lord has forgiven you, so you also must forgive.

Paul is saying that we are to be like Christ—like our King. Using his imagery of taking off the old and putting on the new, I would state the theme of this chapter like this:

---

*A life worthy of the Lord adorns itself*
*in the fashion of the King.*

---

We find the same thought in Ephesians 4, where Paul writes, "Put off your old nature which belongs to your former manner of life, and put on the new nature, created after the likeness of God in true righteousness and holiness."

Ephesians 5 puts it into a Kingdom context by saying, "Be imitators of God. Walk in love as Christ loved us. Be sure of this, that no immoral or impure man, or one who is covetous has any inheritance [note what follows] in the kingdom of Christ and of God."

Using Paul's imagery, I would rewrite the theme of my previous chapter like this: "If a given society is ever to improve, it will be because the spiritual garments worn by the subjects of the great king are obviously far more attractive than what men and women of the world are wearing."

What styles does the world wear? You'll find them listed in Colossians 3. They're obvious things, like immorality—which in Greek means "Illicit sexual intercourse," or as the King James translation reads, "fornication."

There is impurity—which is broader than immorality. It means moral dirtiness, a popular style of the world, but one in which the king's servants should never be seen.

There are passion, evil desires, a lustful mind and covetousness. (Again, commentators agree that the Greek word used here implies covetousness—that is, wanting what belongs to someone else—in the area of sexuality.)

So it looks like the styles of the ancient world didn't differ much from our own times!

In Ephesians 6:8 Paul writes: "On account of these the wrath of God is coming. In these you once walked when you lived in them. But now, put them all away." In other words, they are not compatible with the Kingdom lifestyle and cannot be the spiritual clothing of Christians.

There are other popular styles that relate to the temper—anger, wrath and malice. Put these off too. Anger is a slow, steaming pot, always simmering, unlike wrath, which is like an explosion. The word wrath in Greek connotes a dry stack of straw to which a match has been set. Malice is an active ill will, that, unlike anger or wrath, is a careful and calculated working out of your displeasure. Paul's point is that Kingdom members should never put on filthy garments such as these.

You get the idea. Paul's final two negative categories are sins of the tongue, that is, slander, foul talk from your mouth, lying; and divisions between believers, those things that allow for distinctions, walls, barriers between people. In the Kingdom, writes Paul, "There cannot be Greek or Jew, circumcised or uncircumcised, slave or free man."

But Paul doesn't just show what kind of spiritual clothing the world wears. In the next section (Colossians 3:12-17) he discusses the kind of styles we, as the King's people, should be adorned with—like compassion, a desire to help those in need; and kindness—similar to compassion but broader, implying generosity to all men. His word-picture here is that we should be like wine mellowed with age, vintage wine with no harshness in it.

He lists other styles too, like lowliness and meekness, both of which suggest we should not insist on our own rights. There's patience, which is longsuffering without complaining, and forbearance, which in Greek suggests something like "holding yourself back," "not flying off the handle."

Then there's forgiveness, a kind of test, for as the Lord has forgiven you, so also you must forgive. Or put another way: As the King wore the mantle of forgiveness, so must we.

Verse 14 sums it up: Above all these put on love, which binds everything together in perfect harmony. Verse 25 adds peace, which means peace within the Body of Christ, and verse 15 advises us to wear thankfulness as well.

Although there's not space enough to give a detailed description of every style, let me summarize a few points:

We are not to simply wear one outfit over another, nor should we change back and forth. Instead we should get rid of the old and put on the new.

We should take off malice—the calculated getting even—and put on forgiveness.

We are to take off impurity—moral dirtiness—and put on the pure love of Christ.

We must take off covetousness—craving that which belongs to others—and wear thankfulness for what we have.

The clothing with the print of the stewing, simmering pot—that's anger—is to be tossed aside, and in its place we are to wear the vintage, mellowed wine print of kindness.

Off comes passion, hot and sticky, and we don cool meekness—not demanding.

Take off divisions and distinctions—put on peace and unity.

See what Paul is doing? Like a skilled salesman he's saying, "Come on now, picture yourself in the fashions of the King." Imagine a multi-mirrored view of yourself in something other than grubbies. When you live with the King, you can't go around looking like a bum! Especially when you're trying to convince others to experience the incredible privilege you've been granted of adoption into royalty.

I'm not nearly as good a salesman as Paul, but let me try this sales pitch. First, find time today to at least pick out your new outfit—to be alone and decide on what new spiritual clothing you want to sport. Refer to Colossians 3 if that helps.

Second, since part of the fun of wearing new clothes is looking better, decide how long it should be before someone notices you've made a change. Something old has came off; something new has taken its place. For example, somebody should notice that you've given up dirty talk and put on purity of thought within, say, four weeks at the most.

So say nothing to anyone about the new wardrobe you have picked out. But pray that within the time period determined, you will appear so different, someone will make a positive comment affirming you on your appearance!

Will you try it?

No longer quarrelsome but a peacemaker.

Not untrustworthy but dependable.

Lazy, no; industrious, yes.

Off with evil habits, on with an attitude of victory.

Off with hatred, on with love.

Off with your thoughts, on with God's thoughts.

Off with old clothes, on with new.

Imagine yourself in an original design fashioned by the custom tailor! Fresh garments of righteousness. And such a new spiritual outfit is available to all.

Remember: A life worthy of the Lord adorns itself in the fashion of the King.

Wow—would you look nice!

~

*Oka remembered Mercie's cottage. She remembered the singing at Great Celebration. And she was sorry, suddenly very sorry to have eaten so many of the sweetsounds herself. Clearing her throat, she announced, "I will sing the King's Songs."*

*With that the musicians began to play. Hero lifted a hand to Thespia to help her from the dais, so that in stepping down she would not trip over any of the Lost Children crowded on the floor.*

*Oka began to sing, and her notes dropped out of her mouth most wondrously. But now the people of the Song Studio made sure the hungry ones got first pick and that the rest of the sweetsounds were gathered up in baskets to be taken through the city streets.*

**From the *Tales of the Restoration* story:**
**"The Song Studio"**

CHAPTER 11

# THE WORLD-CHANGERS

~

SOME YEARS AGO I heard an interview with Federico Fellini, the Italian film director. He was responding to critics who said his latest film depicting the ancient Roman world was degenerate. "No," he insisted, "It's exactly the opposite. I was attempting to show viewers the awfulness of the Roman world prior to the sweetness and beauty and transforming power of Christ."

I don't know Fellini's motives for making such a statement. But I think many of us forget the immense changes that came about as a result of the ever-increasing influence of Christ's Kingdom-members in those early centuries. It was important at that time for the salt to be salt, for Christians to fill the role their King intended them to play—world-changers.

Rather than being influenced by pagans, Christians became the influencers. Because they worked at exemplifying God's standard, they had to understand when to say no to evil, and yes to what God approves of. After all, they reflected their King's continued presence in the world.

His pattern—what He said, how He acted—was to be theirs. As believers they mirrored His image. I like to say they adopted a "Kingdom lifestyle." They adorned themselves in the spiritual fashions of their King. And as a result, the world began to change.

But Kingdom members were also characterized by power. I sense that power is a difficult word for present-day believers to grasp. The very term seems to border on magic. If you say you have spiritual power, people expect you to be like a wizard and dazzle them. That idea is fostered, I suppose, by sincere individuals who are overwhelmed by our Lord's miracles and truly want that kind of Christlike power for their own lives.

In fact, many in our society seem to have been bitten by the bug of the spectacular. If the Church only discovered how to match Yoda's tricks in Star Wars, or if Christians could rival the special effects of movies like *Avatar*. "Wow, that's real power!" the neighborhood kids told me after seeing that movie.

The truth is that "real power" in Scripture relates to getting Kingdom work done. Whether it makes people's jaws drop in amazement or their eyes bug out in surprise is immaterial. Don't misunderstand. I'm not saying spiritual power isn't real. It is. And Jesus promises that it is. Paul too wrote in Ephesians 1:18-20, "I'm praying that you may know ... what is the immeasurable greatness of his power [so great is that power that you can't even measure it!] in us who believe, according to the working of his great might which he accomplished in Christ when he raised him from the dead."

But again, what is this power for? It's to advance the Kingdom! Christ Himself makes this connection when He says in Acts 1:8, "You shall receive power ... and you shall be my witnesses to the ends of the earth."

So this is another aspect of the Kingdom lifestyle. We know already it means right-living, or righteousness, loving God, and loving others. Romans 14:17 says, "For the kingdom of God means righteousness and peace and joy in the Holy Spirit."

But living the Kingdom lifestyle also means demonstrating power in relationship to the cause so the King is able to continue His work through us. In that regard, take note of 1 Corinthians 4:15, 18-20, where Paul pens his famous lines about the Kingdom of God not consisting of talk but of power: "For though you have countless guides in Christ, you do not have many fathers. For I became your father in Christ Jesus through the gospel. ... Some are arrogant as though I were not coming to you. But I will come to you soon, if the Lord wills, and I will find out, not the talk of these arrogant people, but their power. For the kingdom of God does not consist in talk but in power."

What is Paul really saying? That he is going to come and cast a spell on the impostors and turn them into toads? I don't think so. He is saying, simply, "When I come, we'll compare lives and see through whom Christ the King is really doing his work!" We can summarize it this way:

*People who live the Kingdom lifestyle demonstrate real power as the King continues His work through them.*

Many years ago I began to write down ways I felt the Kingdom advanced each day as a result of my being a servant of the King. Like a daily report of each day's accomplishments. For instance, "Encouraged Eddie in his walk of faith; ... feel the broadcast I recorded had eternal value; ... showed hospitality to a Christian who needed a place to stay."

As simple as it may sound, this exercise helps me determine my value to the cause. Try it for yourself; it won't take long to find out how much Kingdom power you are using. If, in the course of a given week, the most significant item on your list is "participated in a Sunday School class discussion," then your service is probably mostly talk.

I fear that for many Christians, their faith is mostly words. There seem to be many who love to poke fun at the peculiarities of those they call zealots; they criticize their lack of tact, their insensitivity, their sledgehammer tactics. But in truth, the zealots probably have more to report each evening than do the armchair experts who think they have figured out everything they need to know about the Kingdom.

Paul talks specifically of his critics and contrasts them with himself (1 Corinthians 4). How would you characterize yourself according to Paul's words?

> Already you have become rich. Without us you have become like kings! And would that you did reign, so that we might share the rule with you. ... We are fools for Christ's sake, but you are wise in Christ. We are weak, but you are strong. You are held in honor, but we are in disrepute. ... When reviled, we bless; when persecuted, we endure; when slandered, we try to conciliate; we have become and are now as the refuse in the world, the offscouring of all things.

> This is how one should regard us, as servants of Christ and stewards of the mysteries of God. Moreover it is required of stewards that they be found trustworthy ... therefore do not pronounce judgment before the Lord comes ... then every man will receive his commendation from God.

Sometimes in the evening I find myself wondering whether I really did anything of significance that day. Did the Kingdom profit from my labors? Am I all talk, or is there power in my life? When I face this question, I pray: "Oh, God, will I ever experience even a fraction of what Paul's writing about when he says I should know the immeasurable greatness of your power working in me, the same power that brought from the dead the lifeless, marred body of the great King himself? Dear Father, in a day that's racing toward judgment, don't let me be content to just enjoy the good life won for me by previous generations. Please give me evidence that you're working through me. I feel so small, so inadequate, so much talk, so little power."

Why don't you try writing down your Kingdom accomplishments each day? From experience, I can testify to its value. In fact, at the risk of being pesty, why don't you start tonight?

~

*By the time both knights were seated on their steeds, the Rangers would all be gone. The lights in the lodge would be dark, but Pumpkin would shout anyway, "Onward! Onward under the banner of the King!"*

*But alas, they never seemed to find the service they sought, for the danger was always over when they reached the scene.*

**From the *Tales of the Kingdom* story:**
**"Two Noisy Knights"**

CHAPTER 12

# PRAYER LESSON NUMBER ONE

~

I'm NOT SURE when it happened, but it was inevitable. If Christ lived in our day and we were privileged to travel with Him, like the twelve apostles were, we'd soon have noticed, just as they did—Christ's relationship with God was far more intimate and powerful than ours.

The disciples concluded that Jesus knew a lot more about praying than they did. Had they not observed Him spending entire nights with His Father? So it is no surprise in Luke 11 when they requested, "Lord, teach us to pray!"

Recognizing their growing interest, Jesus responded with His own Prayer Lesson Number One: "Okay, do it like this…" And He outlined for them what we now call the Lord's Prayer.

Many know this prayer by heart. You may even be part of a congregation that regularly recites it during Sunday morning services. But do you understand the prayer? I think many people decided long ago that somehow Jesus missed it with this one. As good as it sounds put to music, when you set out to actually pray the Lord's Prayer—well, it just lacks something!

At least, I used to think that way. But now I'm convinced that Jesus did us a great service and that truly the best way to learn to pray as He did is to master this prayer. Please realize that this endorsement isn't something I just thought of for the first time when putting this book together. Rather, I have worked hard at making the Lord's Prayer my own, and I have profited immensely from studying it, memorizing it, rewriting it in my own words, and—almost without exception—praying it every day for several decades. Because it's such an integral part of me, I believe that those seriously interested in learning how to pray should make it their own Prayer Lesson Number One.

In learning to pray, we dare not be like children with a new musical instrument. They blow, pound, or make whatever noise they can. Sure, a few simple tunes can eventually be produced that others recognize, at least if we're told the name of the song ahead of time! But wouldn't it be better to learn the skills slowly under the direction of a master teacher?

In the discipline of prayer, Christ Himself is our teacher. And how foolish we would be not to learn His first lesson well.

---

*To pray like Christ, we should work on mastering His first lesson on the subject—the King's Prayer.*

---

"Do it like this," said Jesus. "Start by reminding yourself to whom you are speaking. Say, 'Our Father, who art in heaven, hallowed be thy name.'"

When people complain that prayer is dull, I believe much of their problem is they have no real awareness of who is listening. If, when we came into God's presence, He would allow us to see that He is literally there, I believe it would make a huge difference. The problem is that, according to Scripture, those who were most aware of His presence were overwhelmed. When Isaiah saw the Lord, he moaned, "Oh, woe is me! For I am lost, for I am a man of unclean lips, for my eyes have seen the King, the Lord of Hosts!" In Revelation, the Apostle John heard the voice of the risen Jesus and upon seeing him wrote, "When I saw him, I fell at his feet as though dead." Perhaps we are fortunate God has chosen to spare us such a shock.

That doesn't mean, however, that He is any less present when we pray. So we dare not barge into His courts, make a brief statement of greeting, and then rattle off requests—although that's the normal pattern for many people.

According to Jesus, we need to make appropriate introductory remarks before we speak to God—something like: "Father in heaven, hallowed by thy name. Holy, sacred, is your name Lord, and rightly revered above all others."

How often when praying do we take time to weigh our words? We should begin with a carefully worded comment, like: "Father, I kneel as I speak to you, for I am truly humbled by your greatness and by my personal unworthiness to be here apart from your grace."

"Familiarity breeds contempt!" said Aesop. Has the present generation of praying believers become too familiar with their God?

Though not what we would call a personal request, the next part of Christ's prayer lesson was, "Thy kingdom come, thy will be done on earth as it is in heaven." The two phrases mean nearly the same thing. To say, "God I want your kingdom to come," is to say, "I want your will to be done on earth even as it is in heaven!"

By now my words about the Kingdom should be making more sense. As I said before, the Kingdom is any situation where (1) Christ is recognized as King, (2) His will is obeyed, and (3) the king's obedient subjects reap the benefit of that arrangement. That's the way things are in heaven. This part of Jesus' prayer lesson, then, is a prayer for the earth to be a situation where those three conditions will become a reality—just as they are in heaven. So in a sense, it's a prayer for the restoration, the fulfillment of all things in Christ, and the return of the King in power.

It is interesting, isn't it, how quickly the matter of the Kingdom comes up in our Lord's first prayer lesson? After we have introduced our prayer by reminding ourselves to whom it is we are speaking, then we talk to Him about His Kingdom.

But the Kingdom is not just in the future. It is also with us now whenever men and women by faith bow to Christ as King, live in obedience to His will, and reap the present and future benefits of that arrangement. So this prayer also becomes a renewal of one's personal commitment, a kind of pledge of loyalty. "'Father, thy kingdom come, I want your will to be done on earth as it is in heaven.' That's where I am in my allegiance right now!"

You know, it annoys me how many prayers contain personal requests of one kind or another while the Kingdom is totally left out. And I mean totally. What Jesus does for us in this prayer lesson is to establish priorities. When talking to God, He is saying, Kingdom concerns take precedence over everything else. How many of us need to learn this!

Let me offer a challenge. Make the Lord's Prayer your own, and I guarantee the Kingdom vision will always be a priority. The Teacher made sure of that in Lesson Number One.

After this introduction, the prayer lesson shifts to more personal matters. "Give us this day our daily bread"—which is another way of saying, "Please God, supply my basic needs today." As you pray the prayer, name what those needs are: money for food, skill to get along today with your boss, wisdom about a decision that needs to be made. "Father, supply these basic needs, please."

"And forgive us our debts, as we also have forgiven our debtors," Jesus continues. Now, I find forgiving far more pleasant to preach about than to practice. It is even easier to ask, "Would you please forgive me?" than to say to God, "All right, I'll forgive him." When someone has hurt me, I tend to keep score, nurse wounds, or attempt to get even. That's easy to get away with until I come to my daily time of praying the Lord's Prayer. Then all of a sudden I'm in trouble. "Forgive me, Father, in the same way I'm willing to forgive others."

We'll look further at the Lord's Prayer in the next chapter. But for now, I want you to take seriously the challenge of making this prayer your own. Not just the words, as though to recite them each day works some kind of spiritual hocus-pocus. But the ideas, the concepts, the truths the words convey—these are filled with the living Christ Himself.

Say the prayer in your own words. How would you express the ideas behind, "Lead us not into temptation, but deliver us from evil"? "Thine is the kingdom"—how would you rephrase that? Why is the word "glory" included in the closing line?

Work on this prayer. Through constant use allow it to become a part of your being, and more and more you will become like Jesus—like the King Himself—intimate with God and powerfully filled with His Spirit.

∼

*By day these grandmas (and hundreds of others, two for every block) were grey-haired ladies with slightly stooped backs, or soft comfy tummies, or saggy arms, or wrinkled faces. In daylife, all were grannies who doted on their grandchildren. They said, "Of course, dear," to their husbands. They baked endless batches of walnut-chip molasses cookies and kept their houses in immaculate order. But at night, when their grandpa husbands were sleeping after a full day of labor for the Restoration, at night when danger was most near, when dark things dared invade the City of the King, slipping through cracks in the holy Surround, then these grannies became—who would have thought it?—the fierce Granny Vigilantes!*

**From the *Tales of the Restoration* story:
"Granny Vigilantes"**

CHAPTER 13

# TEN MAGIC WORDS

❧

IN THIS CHAPTER I want to share some magic words—ten, to be exact. If used regularly they are guaranteed to be a potent medicine for healing wounds—whether inflicted by a Christian or a non-Christian.

You see, I have been in the battle of the kingdoms long enough to realize not all the distress people experience is a direct result of their own actions. I have wept with husbands whose wives left them for other men. I've counseled adults who painfully recall early physical and psychological scars rendered by unloving parents or guardians. I have heard enough stories from fellow clergy about the insensitivity of parishioners, and I know from my own mistakes how ministers often deeply disappoint their people. Employers have complained to me about their employees' attitudes, and I have heard employees gripe about their employers. Young or old, whatever race, gender, or denomination—you name it—everyone has conflicts. Where there are people, injuries will be found as well.

Now if you hurt but know you are responsible for your own pain, that's one thing. But if someone else has taken advantage of you—well, you are in the group that needs these ten magic words.

Most of us have a rather well-defined sense of justice. If another party has hurt us, we feel their responsibility ought to be admitted. Usually a verbal acknowledgment is adequate. "I'm really sorry," we want people to say. "Is there anything I can do to make it right?" Just to know such words have been sincerely spoken is payment enough. But when no such recognition is forthcoming, we get upset. "Hey, wait a minute!" we cry. "The scales aren't balanced yet. This isn't right!"

For children, everything is easier. You can call the person a name, shove him around if he's smaller, or at least take your toys and march home in a huff. But for adults, society tends to frown on a sharp rap on the nose as a proper way of settling accounts. Getting even, therefore, is more complicated. The normal pattern is to make a mental note that there's a score to be settled, a "collectable" with "payment due" written all over it. And you just wait for the appropriate occasion to collect.

If this sounds familiar, pay attention, because all too often the attitude I'm describing has a price tag on it—one more exorbitant than you may realize. What is most unfortunate about injured people who decide to "bide their time until…" is that such a mindset usually plays havoc with their relationship with God. How hard it is to love and honor the Father while being angry with a brother or sister.

That is why Scripture advises us never to avenge ourselves, but rather to leave such matters to the wrath of God. Too often I've observed even strong Kingdom members getting sidetracked on this kind of thing. Let me put into a sentence what I have in mind:

*Release from the disabling effects of pain caused by others is found through practicing forgiveness.*

Certainly that means practicing forgiveness when asked. You recall Christ's Kingdom parable about the servant who owed his king 10,000 talents. Since a talent equaled about fifteen years of pay for a worker, we're talking about wages for fifteen years times 10,000. Forgiven this massive debt by his king, the servant still refused to show mercy to someone who owed him a sum equal to the wages of a worker for about a hundred days. A good-sized debt, of course, but it was nothing compared to what had just been forgiven him. He too should have practiced forgiveness—like his king!

"Now," said Jesus, "my heavenly Father will reverse his previous stand, put such a one in jail, and make him pay everything if he doesn't forgive his brother from his heart." Read it yourself in Matthew 18. We must forgive when asked.

But we must also forgive even when not asked—just as Christ did when on the cross. "Father, forgive them," He said, "for they don't understand what they're doing."

Thank the Lord that forgiveness doesn't have to be determined by whether or not the offending party asks to be forgiven! Because many won't. And beyond that, the one who wronged you may be dead now. But you need not remain their victim, because you can still forgive them.

Webster defines the word forgive as "To give up claim to requital on account of an offense; to give up resentment; to remit the penalty of a wrong." So when I say that release from the disabling effects of pain caused by others is found through practicing forgiveness, I'm talking about canceling any thought that, to make the matter right, this person is really going to have to "cough up" and be sorry.

Rather, by a Christlike act of love, you (the offended party) decide to declare the payment due is being canceled by you. In other words, although you remember what happened, by an act of your will you choose to declare nothing is now owed. You are taking the due bill and marking it PAID. As you do this, in turn, you will find release from the pain you have suffered. And this is not just theory, either. The pain will literally go away. I have seen it work time and again in people's lives and more than once tested it in my own as well.

To be effective, this cancellation needs to be worked out in prayer before Christ Himself. In His presence, you might want literally to make out a bill reflecting what you feel would be just recompense. You might be thinking, *That cheat owes me at least twenty grand for the idea he stole.* I suggest you do it in Christ's presence because it's harder to overcharge when you remember the Lord also saw everything that happened. "Let's see, God," you might say, "To the best of my memory, this is what took place and what I rightfully feel I have coming." Sometimes, this simple review will end the entire matter. When going over the past before Christ, I am forced to be honest and can tell when I have made more of something than I should have.

But before officially writing VOID on the debit sheet, it's important to take a moment to ask your King whether He can empathize with what you are about to do. Has He had to forgive others for those same hurts? For example, have you suffered physical abuse? Christ did also. Were you betrayed by a close friend? The Monarch also understands what that is like. Maybe you were rejected by leadership in the religious community. So was He. Were you humiliated by exposure of your nakedness? He was as well.

My point is that Christ can identify with your feelings. And He practiced forgiveness!

So when you commit the matter to Him in prayer, you are talking with someone who knows what it is to say, "I choose to cancel this specific debt."

In fact, now is the time to tell you the ten magic words, because they came from the King Himself. You already know them—by heart, but it's possible you didn't realize how effective they were in releasing people from the persistent throb of wounds caused by others. I know you'll recognize them: *"And forgive us our debts as we forgive our debtors."*

To put the idea in other words, you could say: "Because I want to be forgiven for the times I've hurt you, your Majesty, I will forgive those who have hurt me."

Just ten words, but they are filled with magic! As you learn to put these words from the great King's prayer into practice, you're home free, my friend—healed, released, discharged from years of pain.

Here's the prescription: Say the words. Crumple the bill, toss it in the wastebasket, and sleep like a baby. Repeat as often as necessary. These magic words are a balm for wounds of the spirit, and no Kingdom participant should be without them.

∽

*Eddie and Benji looked at each other. They looked at the ground. They nodded their heads. Commander was right. They were no longer working together; in fact, they were never really speaking to each other.*

*Ranger Commander, as he was apt to do, waited a long time before speaking again. "That is correct. You have not been working together. Something has come between you. Now, answer me this question. If there is a breach in friendship, and friends miscalculate one another, could that possibly affect the Power Project?"*

**From the *Tales of the Restoration* story:**
**"Power-outs"**

# CHAPTER 14

# VIDEO-GAME CHRISTIANS

❧

VIDEO GAMES are a giant industry, and I can understand why. where else can you assume command of your own fleet of spaceships; destroy approaching enemy rockets, missiles, saucers; scurry for your life; eventually be blown to smithereens—and walk away unharmed for only twenty-five cents? It's an exciting though unreal world.

Unfortunately, the Kingdom involvement of many North American Christians is of the video-game variety. We play it, and yes, it does require a certain amount of attention, but we don't see it as a life-and-death situation, which may be why many believers walk away from their Kingdom assignments expecting only to have sacrificed some small change!

But in the real world, literal battles are fought every day. Real blood is shed by men and women who believe in dreams quite different from ours—in Central America and Eastern Europe, Asia, Africa, and throughout the Middle East. Nor did fun and games characterize past advances of the Kingdom. Those too were marked by dedication, sacrifice and bloodshed.

Loyal servants of the King, of course, don't fight battles the way soldiers in other causes often do—by taking up arms, planting bombs, and assassinating enemy leaders. But this doesn't mean they aren't fighters.

We need to remind ourselves that from the very beginning the Kingdom advance was bathed in blood. It was first announced by the martyr John the Baptist. Do you recall what Christ asked His followers concerning him? "What did you go out in the wilderness to behold? A reed shaken in the wind? Hardly. A man clothed in soft raiment? Behold those who wear soft raiment are in king's houses. Why then did you go out?

To see a prophet? Yes! Know this, that from the days of John the Baptist until now the kingdom has suffered violence. And men of violence take it by force."

You might disagree, but for John the Baptist, whose head would soon be axed from his body, I am sure Christ's words were meant as follows: "From its inception, John, from its first announcement by you—the Kingdom has been subjected to violence. As a prisoner you will know this. Men of violence attack it by force. We are involved in a clash of powerful kingdoms."

Not only would John have understood Christ's words in this way, but I'm confident Stephen, the first Christian martyr, would have as well. He was pelted with heavy rocks. What more violent scene can you imagine than seeing someone stoned to death? "Quick! he's down," the crowd might have shouted. "He can't protect himself! Another direct hit!" The stones came fast and furious—and they were aimed to kill. If such a scene took place in front of your house, it would make you sick.

Paul faced just such a mob in Lystra—people with rocks in hand to express their hate. They even thought they killed Paul, but before long he bravely and miraculously returned to strengthen the disciples. Exhorting them to continue in the faith, he warned them that "Through many tribulations we must enter the kingdom of God."

Apparently being a victim of violence is not an uncommon Kingdom experience. As Paul says in 2 Thessalonians 1:5, Kingdom members are "being made worthy of the kingdom of God through suffering." What does he mean? Are we suffering if our budget is too stretched to purchase the latest CD by our favorite Christian artist? No. Obviously Paul is talking about matters of substance. "We boast of you in the churches of God," he writes, "for your steadfastness and faith in all your persecutions and in the afflictions which you are enduring."

Although Paul lived in a different time and in a different setting, I still believe whenever the great kingdoms of light and darkness clash—even today—real battle is waged, real wounds are experienced, and real heroic sacrifices need to be made. Some will come out hurting—suffering—because of what this battle costs.

Or is Kingdom involvement like a video game? Are the disasters merely sound effects and computerized pictures of make-believe explosions?

Ask Christ. That's why He made statements like these from Matthew 10:

"Do not fear those who kill the body but cannot kill the soul, rather fear him who can destroy both soul and body in hell. ... Do not think I have come to bring peace on earth, I have not come to bring peace but a sword. For I have come to set a man against his father and a daughter against her mother. He who loves father or mother more than me is not worthy of me, and he who does not take up his cross and follow me is not worthy of me."

Of course you must consider such statements in light of the fact that our King had to bear a cross. He walked the route that led directly to where the enemy was waiting. He chose the path of combat and was first to inflict damage on the spoiler in his very lair. Christ did this alone—and paid dearly for it with His blood.

So it's from such a posture that He demands more than personal comfort and ease from those who fill His ranks.

---

*To be worthy of the King, we too must take up the cross.*
*We must choose the way of spiritual combat,*
*walking the route that leads to the front.*

---

That means the myths that spiritual warfare is gentlemanly, that you enter and leave essentially unscathed, that it costs relatively little, that violent men no longer want to take the Kingdom by force—these myths must forever end.

We cannot be like little boys playing with toy soldiers. They knock them over, run them down, make noises that mean they have been blown to bits—only to arrange them anew the next time they want to play. Rather, as troops who have known the front lines, aware of the dangers, even bearing real bodily wounds, we must return to the battle again and again because we believe in the King and His Kingdom.

How about you? What is your mindset? If you choose to follow the example of your King, then you will think daily in terms of the battle and consciously commit yourself to the role that will best advance Christ's Kingdom and thwart the purpose of the enemy. It's not a casual thing. It's a calculated involvement of yourself and your resources to the cause.

This kind of involvement is more than saying, "Let's see, where do I send what money the Lord has coming this time?" Rather, we should prayerfully ask, "O Lord, help me to put the best I can give to the Kingdom need that's most strategic—even if it hurts."

For a pastor or a teacher, Kingdom involvement is more than thinking, "Where can I find a new devotional thought or illustration to share with these people?" Instead, the attitude should be: "Father, I desperately need to know what you would say if you were to preach here this Sunday. Nothing less will satisfy me. The time is too crucial. The enemy goes from victory to victory. What can I say to hinder him?"

Our prayer cannot be, "Lord, if an opportunity to witness comes, help me to take it," because the opportunity seldom comes, and when it does, we seldom take it. Rather, we must pray for words that burn in our hearts, and we must pray for a place to share them for the sake of the King who is not willing that any should perish.

If you live with any of the intensity I am describing, you will already have experienced the enemy. Don't misunderstand me, though. Encountering violence from the opposition is not a prize to seek. Don't pray for it! It's not an honor I'm anxious to have bestowed on me, even though as a believer it is part of my heritage.

At the same time, however, we should not always equate cross-bearing with nothing more than personal pains and disappointments. Suffering is more than having to put up with lack of appreciation, insult, delay or loneliness.

"War is hell," says the real soldier.

"That was fun! Let's do it again," says the video-game player.

Which are you? In these last days I believe the greatest battle in the clash of the kingdoms has already begun. If you simply want to record your initials as one of the top three scorers at spiritual Pac-Man, then the Kingdom doesn't need you. What it needs is people who are willing to get involved and fight the real battles to the end.

*And Big Operator was glad; his heart leaped with gladness. He knew the Enchanter would take revenge, but even if this was to be his final strategic rescue design ever, he had been at the side of his King as together they emptied the pavilion of every last orphan. He closed his eyes and listened to the taxi vanguard, his taxi vanguard, honking throughout all of Enchanted City.* **HARNK! HARNK!**—*here, there and everywhere*—**HARNK! HARNK!** *It sounded in his ears like a raucous chorus of jubilant rescue.*

**From the *Tales of the Resistance* story:
"The Orphan Exodus"**

# CHAPTER 15

# THE UGLY APOSTLES

~

T HERE'S A VAST DIFFERENCE between a college student and a foreign ambassador representing our country abroad. Worlds apart, wouldn't you say? Well, with that contrast in mind, you can understand the difference between the terms disciple and apostle.

The word disciple actually means "student"—a student of a teacher. In the New Testament the disciples were students of the royal teacher Christ. Apostles, on the other hand, were "commissioned ones," "sent ones," or as Paul, an apostle himself, puts it in 2 Corinthians 5, "Ambassadors for Christ." What do apostles do? Paul defines their role this way: "God making his appeal through us." In other words, apostles are here in His place and on His behalf.

You can see the terms disciple and apostle aren't exactly interchangeable. Keeping this difference in mind helps us to understand the occasion, given in the tenth chapter of Matthew, when Christ summoned His twelve disciples and gave them authority, and then later, when the specific names of the twelve are then listed, these men are referred to as apostles—those who will now be sent out as Christ's official representatives.

All true Christians should be disciples—students—of the teacher Jesus. But not all are called to be apostles, even though in a sense all of us are commissioned to His service and have the authority of the Spirit resting upon us. But there is one aspect of apostleship that not all possess.

Let me illustrate. I receive many letters from men and women in business who want to be more involved in ministry. It's not that they aren't serving Christ already or that they simply want to spend more time directly involved with Kingdom matters. Rather, they feel a need to be commissioned, to be set apart, to be given special authority for such service by the church, just as I, a minister, have been.

So when pressures mount, when deadlines rest heavily on me, when requests for help are beyond my limited resources, when support is lacking, when another trip is scheduled and I'd rather be home with my family, when criticism comes, when opposition is all too obvious—then I am reminded of the privilege I have. I have been singled out in a special way as an official representative of the greatest King in all the world. I need to recognize that I have been called by God and ordained by the church. Not many are granted that opportunity. Not everyone is called to be a leader.

This chapter is for leaders in the King's service, those who are apostles as well as disciples. When Christ returned to His Father, He knew He would have to entrust His Kingdom into others' hands. Leaders would be necessary. And a corollary to leadership is the authority commensurate with the responsibility.

Such Kingdom positions are not that easy for mere humans to fill. But who—understanding the true identity of the King, the grand purpose of His Kingdom, and the ultimate realities involved—would say to Christ's invitation, "No, I'm not interested!"? The disciples left their nets, a lucrative job at a tax table, and other pursuits because they were being called to something bigger and more exciting than they had ever known. Having said all that, let me share with you the key sentence for this chapter:

*Leaders privileged to represent the Kingdom should pattern their involvement after the model of their King.*

If there is a group of people anywhere who should reflect what the King and His Kingdom stand for, certainly His commissioned ones, those officially recognized as the leaders in His cause, should be that group. And that is not my idea; Christ Himself said so. "It is enough," He declared in Matthew 10:25, "for the disciple to be like his teacher, and the servant like his master."

Do you recall the book The Ugly American? First published in the sixties, it was one of the best exposés of why the rest of the world didn't seem to think as highly of Americans as we ourselves did. Its premise was that the lifestyle of the people in the U.S. diplomatic service made us appear ugly, and this needed to be changed.

By calling this chapter "The Ugly Apostles," I am questioning whether those of us called to represent the greatest of all kings would not be wise to emulate what the King Himself stood for. Could it be the image of today's Kingdom ambassadors is less than it should be?

Fortunately, Christ gave us some information as to what His ambassadors should be like. Let me share some of His concerns about his representatives—about the men and women commissioned specifically for His service—about all today who have been set aside for Kingdom work.

First, do we represent Christ well by the message we preach? Jesus preached the good news of the Kingdom. Luke 9:2 says, "He sent them out to preach the kingdom of God." Is this still the message being proclaimed by His servants?

Second, do we represent Christ well by our lifestyles? Jesus' lifestyle was one of simplicity. To those He sent out to represent His cause He said, "You received without pay, give without pay. Take no gold, nor silver, nor copper in your belts, no bag for your journey, nor two tunics, nor sandals, nor a staff; for the laborer deserves his food." A literal interpretation is not intended here; at least, American ministers don't wear sandals and carry a staff. But the intent is to portray a lifestyle of simplicity, one in which the honorarium or the salary is not the bottom line. The emphasis is not on a new outfit for every occasion, facilities that stagger the imagination, the diamond stickpin approach—no! The focus must be on how to accomplish the task at hand with the least number of complicating factors.

Third, do we represent Christ well by the authority we bear? Jesus knew the enemy was subject to Him. He had total confidence in the words He spoke. He taught as one who had authority. Did He not say, "All authority in heaven and on earth has been given to me"? When He set aside the Twelve, He gave them authority over unclean spirits, to cast them out, and to heal every disease and every infirmity. The seventy also returned joyfully saying, "Lord, even the demons are subject to us in your name." Do ministers carry this kind of authority with them today? Most of the time, I fear not—and I'm part of the group I'm criticizing. And incidentally, a powerful personality is not the same thing as authority!

Fourth and last, do we represent Christ well by the warfare we wage? John writes, "The reason the Son of God appeared was to destroy the works of the devil." In Matthew 10 and Luke 9 and 10, where it speaks of setting aside people for service, the theme of spiritual warfare is addressed: "When they persecute you in one town, flee to the next"; "Behold, I send you out as sheep in the midst of wolves"; "Do not fear those who kill the body but cannot kill the soul"; and so on.

People in ministry cannot rest content just to be thought of as part of a respected profession. It's imperative that we think beyond career and honors and personal comfort and retirement. In the cosmic conflict between light and darkness, God's Kingdom and Satan's, we are officers in the cause of Christ the great King.

I would like to challenge you who are fellow "called-out" ones. You are students, yes, but you are more. You are apostles—not like the original twelve, perhaps, but commissioned for God's service nonetheless. Read Matthew 10 and Luke 9 and 10, and ask yourself, *Do I represent Christ the way I should? By the message I preach? Does the Kingdom dream live in me? By the lifestyle I live? Am I bogged down in my service because of too much baggage? By the authority I bear? In my mind am I aware of the true power and glory of the one I serve? By the warfare I wage? Is the clash of the kingdoms real to me or imaginary?*

We dare not be ugly apostles. We might be ugly ducklings, perhaps—strange to the outside world but beautiful to those in the know. But not ugly apostles!

The Apostle Paul was very much like the Lord in what he preached, the simple lifestyle he lived, the authority he bore, the warfare he waged. Yet even Paul asked, "Who is sufficient for these things?" "But we are not like so many," he continues, "mere peddlers of God's word: but as men commissioned by God, in the sight of God we speak in Christ!"

And so must we.

~

*"Baker, it is you who has wounded me, even you."*

*The Chief Baker fell to his knees. "Not I, my lord! Not I!" But he knew it was true. He was haunted by a face and by eyes and by a cry. He had given one dirt, one stones, and the other beatings.*

**From the *Tales of the Kingdom* story:**
**"The Baker Who Loved Bread"**

CHAPTER 16

# KEEPERS OF THE KEYS

~

THE KINGDOM PASSAGE examined in this chapter is one of the most controversial in the Bible. In Matthew 16:19, Jesus says to Peter, "I will give you the keys to the kingdom of heaven and whatever you bind on earth will be bound in heaven, and whatever you loose on earth will be loosed in heaven." Just what He meant has been questioned for centuries.

To avoid the doctrinal squabbles that have often sidetracked the study of this passage, I want to examine it from a practical vantage-point. This way maybe we can get more quickly to the heart of what Christ meant.

Suppose a king of incredible wealth desires to do something of value for his people—let's say he decides to put millions of dollars into building a magnificent public garden. Even though no expense will be spared, admission will be free and no one will be excluded.

Why all this generosity? Because the giver wants people to be happy, to know joy, to experience the best of what life has to offer. He wants them to live at least partially on his own level of wealth and abundance.

Of course, certain rules have to be established. For instance, the king will have to be thanked for his kindness, for it would not be good for people to receive so much without a spirit of sincere gratitude. Also, everyone who comes is to follow the loving example of the giver and in turn demonstrate a concern for the wellbeing of others. Nothing that difficult—just rules to ensure maximum benefit for all, so that no one is cheated out of the benefits of the magnificent garden.

So all in all it's a wonderful thing, this garden—except few people know about it, and its gate is locked.

"But to you," says the king, "I entrust the keys. It's obvious that you understand my heart. Take these and do what you should. The future success of this venture rests with you. Now, I must be about other important matters!"

What an honor! What a responsibility!

What would you do? Would you use the keys selfishly? Would you emphasize repeatedly that you alone have the final say as to who is allowed in and who isn't? In a sense that's true—you do have the keys! Or would you let everyone know about this man's benevolence, while at the same time protecting his interests by making known and enforcing the few stipulations he established?

My guess is that this king would be interested in whether or not people were using and enjoying his gift. The importance and power attributed to you, the holder of the keys, would be far less significant to him.

This illustration might be analogous to what's happening in Matthew 16. It implies that our focus should not concern the kind of power Christ did or did not bestow on Peter. Rather, Jesus was talking about something new and wonderful that had come to earth—the Kingdom of God itself and the possibility for everyone to participate in life in a whole new way. So different, however, was this kingdom that people would ruin it if they didn't understand certain basic principles.

What principles? That everybody would have to know who Jesus was— the very anointed one of God Himself. Isn't this what Peter had just said? "You are the Christ [the Messiah, the anointed one, the king himself], the Son of the living God!"

---

*To enter the Kingdom, then, all must first kneel before Christ. Once in the Kingdom, all must live in the fashion of the King.*

---

For people to live as they had previously would destroy the true wonder of the gift. So the person holding the keys was not only to open up this marvel, but to protect it from ruin as well.

"You understand me, Peter," Christ seemed to be saying. "You are someone to whom I can entrust the keys to my Kingdom!"

"Oh, let me see the keys, Peter, let me see 'em!" begged John immediately. That's in verse—well, at least it's in the verse I just made up! But it does point to the fact that the keys were not literal, but a figure of speech.

At this point you might say, "But David, consider the verse that follows: 'Whatever you bind on earth shall be bound in heaven, and whatever you loose on earth shall be loosed in heaven'—sounds like the keys were much more than just a casual remark."

Perhaps so. But you must realize this whole incident isn't even mentioned in the other gospels. And those identical words about binding and loosing are spoken by Christ again just two chapters later (Matthew 18:18), when He's talking then to all His disciples. Check it out. It would seem then that they too must have been given keys.

But again, what was Christ's intent with His comment about the keys? Was it to let everyone know clearly who was in charge of letting people into the Kingdom and keeping them out? I don't think so. If anything, it was a charge to see to it that the wonders of the Kingdom would be open to all, but not so indiscriminately its uniqueness could be destroyed.

Of course the question that follows is, *Was Peter a good key-keeper?* And that's in light of Christ's interest in whether or not people were enjoying and profiting by the gift He had given the earth. What was happening with this alternative kingdom—this place where those who mourn find comfort, those who hunger and thirst for righteousness discover it, and the pure in heart see God? Was this key-keeper opening up this special world for all, and was he making sure that Kingdom principles were being adhered to?

Or was Peter more interested that people know about the great power he himself had—to give or withhold that which they longed for? My feeling is that Peter proved worthy of this honor. There's no mention of keys in his two epistles, but he does write repeatedly about the wonders of who we are in Christ and the need for us to live in accord with His desires.

If someone was like Peter, do you think Christ would designate him a key-keeper too? Like John or Paul maybe? Weren't these men also given the keys to the Kingdom? Unlike the Pharisees about whom Jesus said, "You shut the kingdom of heaven against men; for you neither enter yourselves, nor allow those who would enter to go in"—all the disciples, save Judas, were Kingdom-proclaimers and enforcers of Christ's desires. And to each of them Jesus said when they received the Spirit, "If you forgive the sins of any, they are forgiven, if you retain the sins of any, they are retained."

What do you think Christ would say today to someone who, like Peter, attempted to draw people to the wonder of the Kingdom on the King's terms? Would He state, "That's nice, friend. But, you see, Kingdom keys can't be handed out to just anyone!"?

Or would he say this: "I'm always looking for people like you. A set of Kingdom keys is yours. Now, raise your right hand and repeat after me:

*"It is my earnest desire to make known to others the wonders of the Kingdom of God. I am also aware of the need to protect the interests of the Kingdom from that which would destroy its beauty. In the receiving of these keys that literally open to people the magnificence of life as intended by the Creator, I realize that I have been entrusted with something of great value. It is my pledge not to use this privilege for selfish interests. Whatever honor it affords me in the minds of others must be accounted for to the Monarch Himself. I hereby pledge myself to the King and to the restoration."*

Such a vow, I realize, does not cover all the ramifications of this passage. But I believe it does capture the practical intent of what holding keys to the Kingdom is all about.

Read the pledge once more. And take a moment to make it your own.

~

*"I am a King's man!" shouted the Ranger. "I have taken the King's vow! I am part of the Watch of the Protectors! You have not judged me rightly. You are mistaken."*

*Mercie's voice was low and sad and gentle. "No, sir. It is you. We have seen."*

*"Repent," said Ranger Commander, his voice rough. "Repent and do penance. The Kingdom will open to you again."*

**From the *Tales of the Kingdom* story:**
**"The Faithless Ranger"**

# CHAPTER 17

# GET BEHIND ME

～

SELF-DENIAL—that's something that most 21st-century Americans have trouble with, isn't it?

Early in his career as an apostle, Peter probably would have fit right in with present-day Christians—he wasn't good at self-denial either. I base this observation on a remark Peter made to Christ. In the last chapter, we looked at his response to Jesus' question, "Who do you say that I am?" Peter answered, "You are the Christ, the son of the living God." Jesus then talked of several matters including giving Peter the keys to the Kingdom.

Strangely enough, following Peter's great declaration that Jesus is God's Son, Christ begins to describe what lies ahead in Jerusalem. He speaks of suffering and death, not a throne and a crown as Peter expected. We find this in Matthew 16, Mark 8 and Luke 9, which are parallel accounts of this incident.

"No!" cried Peter. "God forbid! This must never happen to you!"

But our Lord, more attuned to God's ways, knew otherwise. He understood that before the Kingdom could become a reality, men and women would have to experience forgiveness from God, release from the enemy, and power to enflesh the new Kingdom lifestyle.

It meant that He Himself would have to be more than their example. He would have to deny His personal desires and accept some very hard things.

So now, as when His ministry began (tempted by the devil in the wilderness and refusing to even toy with the suggestions put before Him), our Lord responds once again quickly and harshly to a suggestion that could have become too attractive if mentally toyed with: "Get behind me, Satan!" he snaps. "You are a hindrance to me; for you are not on the side of God, but of men."

All of this probably would have been just fine if Christ had stopped there, but He didn't! He then said, "If any man would come after me, let him deny himself and take up his cross and follow me."

What kind of monarch was this? I don't think any of us have imagined a king saying, "Before my kingdom can become a reality, I must submit soon to an ignominious death. And anyone who would come after me will also have to deny himself and take up his cross and follow me." Luke went even further—he records that Christ said, "Take up his cross daily"!

Well, it seems to me Jesus was being realistic. Just as there was no way around the cross if the Kingdom was to become a reality, neither was there any way of escaping the need for daily cross-bearing on the part of all who would follow, if its advance was to continue. To fill the ranks with people who would flee at the first sign of opposition and cringe at the thought of personal sacrifice would be useless. One might as well not run the Kingdom flag up the pole. Christ's cause was going to require the ability to stick in there when times got rough.

One of my greatest concerns for Kingdom participants in our day is that we aren't tough enough. We manifest too much the spirit of our age. In North America, we experience the most advantaged society in the history of the world. Much of this has resulted from the self-denial, perseverance and hard work of earlier generations. But somewhere along the line a new god raised his head. His name? The gratification of self.

Undoubtedly this new deity is incredibly attractive. Given the opportunity, who wouldn't want to worship the fulfillment of his or her own desires? Who wouldn't be pleased with what "sin" has become under this new system? Today, by definition, to "sin" is to foolishly restrain one's self in any area of basic emotional need, to allow personal wants to remain unfulfilled. Believing that "You only go around once," our society looks with great suspicion at self-denial.

At least, this is the creed of literally millions upon millions of North Americans. Our culture is in the throes of an incredible revolution of thought that is casting off traditional values and calling not for controls, but for ever-increasing freedom and license, all in the guise of self-actualization.

Have believers been affected? Time after time I see those who say they belong to the Lord choosing not only to condone but embrace what they know to be sin. And they do this in the name of self-realization. Even leaders in the cause say, "My marriage is no longer fulfilling to me; I'll break it and enter another." Often I wonder if a more accurate term might not be self-indulgence. But whatever it is called, it is the opposite of what Christ was talking about.

---

*The Kingdom advances only when its subjects follow their King's practice of daily self-denial.*

---

After Jesus told His disciples, "If any man would come after me, let him deny himself and take up his cross daily and follow me," He added, "For whoever would save his life will lose it and whoever loses his life for my sake, he will save it. For what does it profit a man if he gains the whole world and loses [or forfeits] himself?"

What if Christ had acted differently? What if our Lord had said, "I've had it with the criticism, the pressure, the homeless wanderings, the endless lines of broken humanity wanting healing, the blindness of the religious establishment, the fickleness of the crowds, the need to hide my true greatness. Forget this cross, forget the pain, forget the separation from my Father." What then? Where would that leave you and me?

Or what if in the earlier religious awakenings in this land, our spiritual leaders had acted differently? What if, during the Great Awakening in the 1740s, George Whitefield had said, "I'm tired of traveling, of being so exhausted others have to hoist me into the saddle and send me in the direction of the next waiting crowd, of being so beat they almost have to prop me up to preach, of the long trips across the ocean, of not having any time to court a bride, of the constant criticism. I'm tired of being gracious. Forget this grind, forget the daily cross-bearing!"

Again I ask, where would that leave us?

What if the Kingdom's grand tradition of self-denial and suffering and death stops? Suppose it dies in our generation? What then? What if we, through our self-indulgence, put to rest the Kingdom dream? What about our children and their children, and what about the world? What about our King's desires?

My suspicion is that we need to say much more often, "Get thee behind me, Satan. You are a hindrance to me, for you are not on the side of God, but of man!"

Now some may caution against an overemphasis on self-denial. They fear Christians will separate themselves—become hermits or live in underground caves as happened in eras of the past. But that's the least of my worries. If such an imbalance returns, I'll be one of the first to preach about it. But that's light-years from the problem that faces us right now.

The kind of self-denial I'm talking about should deeply affect our lives. I suggest we examine ourselves in three basic areas that relate to what Christ was talking about: time, money and talents.

How do you use your time? Are you self-indulgent or self-denying? Is television a problem? I ask because statistics say watching TV ranks second only to sleep in terms of time spent per week by the average American. "I only watch three or four hours a week," some might say. But do you give that much time each week to advancing the Kingdom? And which is more important? Do you perceive of your time as yours to do with as you please? That's indulgence! I believe time should be viewed by us as a gift from God to use as a wise and disciplined steward.

How about money? "Brand-new furniture would be nice, but I believe I would do better to invest my money in Kingdom matters"—that's the kind of attitude that's written the history of the Church during all her advancements. Self-denial says, "I could, but I won't for the sake of the King and the restoration." Cross-bearing has a direct relationship to money.

What about your talents and skills? Do you spend hours and hours each week with a camera, gardening, woodworking, or playing golf? There's nothing wrong with such things—unless they become your first love. Eternity will reveal whether you are more wise to have invested your skills in Kingdom matters. When people used their skills and talents for the Kingdom, then new mission fields opened up for the Gospel, ministries of love were established for alcoholics and drug addicts, people were reached for Christ in evangelistic crusades and in one-on-one evangelism, evils like slavery and abortion-on-demand were battled with, great times of spiritual awakening were brought about.

It is the exact opposite of asking, "What's in it for me?" "Is it fun?" "Who gets the credit?"

That's when Jesus said to Peter, "Get behind me, Satan!" Because Peter was voicing words that, if followed, meant the death of the Kingdom dream. And adherence to the spirit of indulgence spells the same thing now—death.

Whoever saves his life will lose it, but whoever loses his life for the sake of Christ and the Kingdom—he will save it. "Come after me," said the King, "Deny yourself, take up your cross daily and follow me."

～

*Close up, Hero could see that when the crowd in the meeting room shouted out these words, a yellow light gleamed in the eyes of the Maestro.*

*"Aha!" he cried. "This is my Song Studio. We will do here what I say!"*

*Suddenly Hero knew what was familiar about the music conductor. This was not a King's man. This was a saboteur, someone who had infiltrated a Safe Place and was actually teaching the people the Enchanter's ways.*

**From the *Tales of the Restoration* story:**
**"The Song Studio"**

CHAPTER 18

# Comparative Riches

～

A NEW MOVEMENT can always benefit from having a few rich and famous converts. So it must have been exciting when a wealthy young man approached Christ to talk about his possible involvement in the Kingdom. I can just hear one of the apostles exclaim, "Wow, this guy is future board-member material!"

Unfortunately, a meeting of the minds didn't happen. The fellow was reluctant to give up his riches. He and Christ came to an impasse on the issue, and the man just walked away sad.

Don't misunderstand. Christ isn't opposed to money, but He wasn't about to be party to the man ending up with fool's gold instead of real gold.

At the beginning of His ministry Christ had said, "Do not lay up for yourselves treasures on earth where moth and rust consume and where thieves break in and steal, but lay up for yourselves treasures in heaven, where neither moth nor rust consumes and where thieves do not break in and steal."

Simply put, He meant material wealth is not a safe bet. Even if a person could hold on to it down here for sixty, seventy, eighty years, there was still no way to transfer it to eternity.

I know some wealthy people. Materially speaking, every single one of them will take into the next world exactly what I do. No more and no less. A totally different system of values is important in God's Kingdom. And not because I say so—the now and future King did! The only true treasure in heaven relates to our Kingdom involvement here. It may be hard to believe, but a cup of cold water given someone today in Jesus' name is of greater worth in this future, unending economy than making a $10 million killing in the stock market.

So be careful, warned Jesus. Don't get involved in the wrong treasure-hunt. He was especially concerned because He knew people get obsessed with such quests. After a while little else matters to them, or as Jesus put it: "Where your treasure is, there will your heart be also."

Or look at it a different way. Where is your mind when it's free to roam? When it's not being paid to be elsewhere, what does it think about again and again? That's the real tip-off as to where your heart is. "What I want," Christ was saying, "for my sake and for yours also, is that it will be drawn to matters of the Kingdom."

"No man can serve two masters," He continued, "for he will be devoted to the one and despise the other." Then He picks out one such master and says, "You cannot serve God and mammon [money]." To put it another way, if you choose the pearl of great price, you can't still want a handful of other pearls as well.

At that point in the story, interestingly enough, Christ was not talking to wealthy people. Since these words came from His Sermon on the Mount, most of those listening were likely poor. I believe Jesus knew that poor people could be as obsessed with money as rich folk.

Even religious leaders can be obsessed with it. Who talks more about money than preachers! Luke, in his parallel passage about serving God and money (16:14-15) reports: "The Pharisees, who were lovers of money, heard all this and they scoffed at him. But he said to them, 'You are those who justify yourselves before men, but God knows your hearts.'"

Now, Jesus didn't mean His followers were to be foolish about money or that He frowned on budgeting, opposed savings accounts, or would be horrified if we considered insurance, and so on. What He *did* mean was that money was not to be our god—that which we made our source of security, that which always captured our thoughts and our conversation, that which gave us delight. These areas were to be filled by the King and His Kingdom vision.

Let's look at the story of the rich young man in Matthew 19 again. What was it that indicated to our Lord that this man's riches were a problem? I don't know. Maybe his talk gave him away. We don't have the whole conversation, but often our words reveal those things our worlds revolve around. Possibly it was his clothing. Did our Lord detect that how he looked had become too important to him? Maybe. In any case, Christ, who knew what was in men's hearts, quickly said to him, in effect,

"The bottom line is going to be which treasure you feel most strongly about. If you really want what you've asked for, you need to sell everything you have before coming with us."

It was a tough request, but not a new one. Nothing more was being required of him than of anyone else. In Matthew 19:27, Peter said quite accurately, "Lo, we have left everything and followed you!" And that was true. Peter and his friends just hadn't had as much to get rid of, that's all!

Another thought: In history, kings have sometimes been notorious for devising ways to cheat their people out of money. Stories such as Robin Hood and his escapades against evil Prince John ride on this theme of calling into account a monarch's insatiable greed for personal luxury. But this wasn't true of Christ. Our good King didn't ask for the proceeds of this man's private sale. He doesn't even say the young man will have to quit treasure-hunting forever. Christ's only concern was that this ruler hunt for those things that were truly valuable, although what Jesus considered valuable was unlike the world's consensus both then and now.

Still, this disciple-candidate couldn't act on what he heard. The Bible says he was sorrowful. Think about that. The dictionary defines sorrowful as "full of sorrow, disappointment, regret, grief." Why was the young man sorrowful? The Scriptures read, "For he had great possessions."

There's a great difference between him and the selfish rich fool who declared, "I have ample goods laid up. So I'll eat, drink, be merry, and lay out plans for bigger barns!" Yet there's also marked similarity in that both chose to put confidence in earthly treasures rather than heavenly ones.

With the perspective of time we can see how unwise they were. Given a choice, we'd much rather be like the disciples who were told at the end of this account, "Truly, I say to you, in the new world, when the Son of Man shall sit on his glorious throne, you who have followed me will also sit on twelve thrones, judging the twelve tribes of Israel. And everyone who has left houses or brothers, sisters, fathers, mothers, children, lands for my sake, will receive a hundredfold [that's not bad!] and inherit eternal life [pretty good deal there too!]. But many that are first will be last and the last first."

There he goes again—turning topsy-turvy what most people accept blindly.

Maybe it's as hard for you to readjust your thinking as it was for the rich young man. If so, I recommend some intense thinking on the subject.

In a sentence, my emphasis can be stated thus:

---

*The decision to value heavenly riches above earthly ones
is a primary Kingdom consideration.*

---

Our Lord seemed to be telling the young man, "You are at a crossroads, friend. You're going to have to make a choice!"

And I'm writing the same thing to you on the King's behalf! Man or woman, Christian worker of long standing or newcomer to the Kingdom, anyone who is caught trying to serve both God and money, here is the message for you: The time has come to make a choice. The King is asking: "Which is it going to be? Treasure in heaven or treasure on earth?"

He asks only because He loves you, for what He said on the subject is the truth—heavenly treasure is more real than what man declares has value. And you know that's so. Do earthly treasures bring lasting joy, or just a temporary illusion of joy?

Still, illusions can be hard to let go of. Jesus said as much. "It will be hard," He stated, "for the rich to enter the kingdom. Again, I tell you, it is easier for a camel to go through the eye of a needle than for a rich man to enter the kingdom of God."

Astonished, the disciples asked, "Who then can be saved?"

To which the King responded, "With men this is impossible. But with God all things are possible."

～

*"How can we ever thank you?" said Carny's mother. Carny thought she was so beautiful with her eyes moist and shining.*

*The young man smiled again, bent, and kissed the palm of Carny's hand, which he then placed beneath the coverlet. "Become a part of the Resistance that is working for the restoration of my Kingdom," he answered. "Throw all your resources into it. But only if you think it's a cause worth living and dying for."*

**From the *Tales of the Resistance* story:
"The Carnival Daughter"**

CHAPTER 19

# THE PEARL OF GREAT PRICE

~

*The kingdom of heaven is like treasure hidden in a field which a man found and covered up. Very excited about his discovery, he inquired as to the cost of the field, but unfortunately found it to be quite expensive. To purchase it he would have to sell all that he had just to raise enough capital. Even so, now he thought he would, but then again, now he thought he wouldn't. Oh, what should he do?! Eventually, continued vacillation wore away the keen edge of his anticipation. So now, he chooses to be content in his knowledge. But then, isn't there a certain sense of security in just knowing where the treasure is?*

*Again, the kingdom of heaven is like a merchant in search of fine pearls, who, on finding one pearl of great value, ceased to look any further for he knew his eyes had seen what was undoubtedly the most beautiful pearl in all the world. … The end.*

"WAIT A MINUTE," you interject, "That's not how I remember those passages! You've changed what the Bible says!" That's right, I did; because when one studies the actual sayings of Jesus, the force of His statements can begin to wear on you. I altered these two parables to make them more palatable. I mean, I get tired of pushing people to line up their lives with what Jesus said all the time.

"That's a dangerous practice!" you warn. "You better be careful with that kind of thing!"

"All right," I respond, "If you want it straight, here it is! But don't say I didn't warn you!" In Matthew 13:44-45 Jesus actually says:

*The kingdom of heaven is like treasure hidden in a field, which a man found and covered up; then in his joy he goes and sells all that he has and buys that field. Again, the kingdom of heaven is like a merchant in search of fine pearls, who on finding one pearl of great value, went and sold all that he had and bought it.*

What do you think Christ hoped to teach by these two Kingdom parables? They are remarkably similar, and since one follows the other, I presume they both make a similar point! Here are two individuals who suddenly discover something that represents the ultimate in value to them. That word ultimate means "beyond which it is impossible to go; the very highest; the absolute maximum." So the merchant in search of fine pearls found one unlike all the rest, and the man in the field had actually discovered treasure!

In fact, they valued these objects so highly that they went and sold all they had to obtain what they wanted. There's not much I can think of for which I'd sell everything to possess. I would sell my car, perhaps; my library possibly; my house—but everything? I don't know! That pearl would have to be worth a king's ransom, wouldn't it?

But then Christ wasn't talking about pearls or treasure chests. He was telling us something important about the Kingdom. He was saying, "What I'm preaching represents the ultimate in value—this actual participation of human beings in the very Kingdom of God or the kingdom of heaven. How are you going to top that? What I'm telling you about represents such inestimable worth that you would be foolish not to exchange all that you have for such a remarkable find."

Christ was saying:

---

*Having discovered that which represents the ultimate in value, one is wise to pursue it at all costs.*

---

In fact, not pursuing it means you are undecided as to its value. It's wise to weigh something carefully before putting everything you have into it. But to be so cautious in your actions, so unable to make up your mind, makes it obvious to all that other matters are now more primary pursuits for you.

Lest you think I'm stretching the point, recall for a moment various occasions when Christ said this same truth even more directly. One doesn't have to figure out the meaning of a parable when you read Christ's words to the circumspect young man in Matthew 19. Do you remember him from the last chapter? He could say to Jesus that he had kept all the commandments. And Christ responded, "Then go sell what you possess and give to the poor, and you will have treasure in heaven, and come, follow me."

Even so, when the young man heard Jesus' words, he went away sorrowful, for he had great possessions. He passed up the pearl. He decided not to buy the field. Unfortunately, it cost more than he wanted to pay. How painful an exchange Kingdom involvement can be for those with great resources—like money, talent, brains, looks or power!

Just one more passage before putting to rest this matter of Christ's strong expectations of those who come upon the Kingdom. Matthew 10:37-39: "He who loves father or mother more than me is not worthy of me; and he who loves son or daughter more than me is not worthy of me, and he who does not take his cross and follow me is not worthy of me. He who finds his life, will lose it." In other words, go after other desires, and they'll vanish just when you think you have them in your grasp. "But he who loses his life for my sake will find it." Restated: The treasure is genuine, worth way more than you ever dreamed. The pearl is truly one-of-a-kind, unique. There's not another like it anywhere, believe me!

"Doesn't it bother you, David," someone asks, "That a reader will take literally what you're writing and, I mean, sell everything just like in the parable—the whole shebang—what then?"

Actually, I'm more concerned with the vast number who say in words but not in their actions that the wishes of the great King come first, when the truth is that actively pursuing Kingdom matters isn't even on their agenda for today. And so what if someone does go overboard, becomes too zealous, thinks of little else? He or she will be in good company!

Back in A.D. 1205, for example, another fine young man turned his back on his inheritance. This fellow sold everything he had, gave the money to the poor and even disowned his father because of the demands of Christ he felt on his life. He was from the Italian town of Assisi. His name was Francis. Even today, over 800 years later, we sing in our churches the prayer he wrote:

*Lord, make me an instrument of thy peace.*
*Where there is hatred let me sow love.*
*Where there is injury, pardon.*
*Where there is doubt, faith.*
*Where there is despair, hope.*
*Where there is darkness, light.*
*Where there is sadness, joy.*
*Lord, grant that I may seek rather*
*To comfort than be comforted.*
*To understand than to be understood.*
*To love than to be loved.*
*For it is in giving that one receives,*
*By forgiving that one is forgiven,*
*And by dying, that one awakens to eternal life.*

Maybe, like some, you think the song is nice as long as no one forces you to take it too literally. Or possibly you believe the treasure in the field is genuine, but you're confused regarding what "selling all" means.

May I suggest that you look at these matters one day at a time. "What will I exchange today for this greater treasure of the Kingdom?" Answer that question and you're on the right path. In time it will take you to where you want to go. What will I exchange today for the greater treasure of the Kingdom? Perhaps I'll exchange my pride for the privilege of sharing with someone about my King. Or I'll exchange this nice but unnecessary purchase to be able to help with a Kingdom advance where the battle is hot. I'll exchange the freedom of my weekends this quarter to reply "Yes" to the question of whether I'll teach the junior-high Sunday School class. I'll exchange privacy and convenience in our home for the honor of seeing Christ work through us in bringing healing to a houseguest who's been badly marred by the world.

Where are you in all this, my friend? Are you like the shopper who finds exactly what is wanted but keeps looking anyway, just in case there's still something better? Be careful that you don't take so long that what you found and liked so much at first is gone when you finally return for it. Today go after the field with the treasure.

Go after the pearl.

Go after the Kingdom.

Pursue it at all costs.

~

After a while she spoke, "Did anyone tell you what Big Operator's last words were when he was taken captive? You'll need it for the Chronicle."

Hero shook his bowed head, and she continued. "He had been badly beaten; three or four Breakers attacked him. Destruction was dismantling his lifework; but as they were dragging him away, he struggled to his feet and called out for all of us to hear above the din, 'the Restoration is near!' They knocked him senseless as he must have known they would. But, Hero, I keep hearing his cry, over and over—'the Restoration is near!'"

**From the *Tales of the Resistance* story:**
**"The Enchanter's Revenge"**

CHAPTER 20

# Choose Your Harvest

∽

R ELIGIOUS LEADERS in Iran must be far more careful about what they say than ministers or priests in America. I believe it's accurate to say that in most Arab countries, political leaders are quite touchy about words spoken out of turn.

When you read the gospels you recognize Christ was in a similar setting. Palestine was occupied by the Romans. Never known for graciousness, the Roman oppressors had an even shorter toleration fuse there than normal. So Jesus, who was followed by vast crowds and whose message concerned an alternative kingdom, had to be extremely guarded about what He said.

Along with being judicious, Christ also had to keep His words simple. His messages were not available in print to be studied. No reporter condensed His words for the next morning's newspaper, and the salient points were not discussed on the evening news. The word about His new Kingdom spread through the people who heard the preacher Himself. And they needed to be able to understand and retain what He said in order to repeat His message to others. To accomplish this, Jesus resorted to a device we call parables.

Parable is composed of two Greek words—para- and ballein—which together mean "To throw or place something alongside something else." Thus, a parable is something that is placed beside something else; or more specifically in Christ's case, a parable takes what is common to our life and puts it alongside a truth about the Kingdom.

In the next several chapters we will look at some of these Kingdom parables. One of the longest and best known is the parable of the sower recorded in Matthew, Mark and Luke.

Your first reaction may be one of disinterest; you've probably heard the story dozens of times. But I guarantee it wasn't dull back in Jesus' day. With talk of Christ on everyone's lips, excitement building about His Kingdom, concern as to possible Roman retaliation, knowing Jesus had to be careful about what He said—I believe the crowds understood His guardedness and actually delighted in trying to figure out what was meant. After all, were they not recipients of important secrets?

Imagine yourself among the multitudes in Matthew 13 that came to hear Him:

*And great crowds gathered around him so that he got into a boat and sat there, and the whole crowd stood on the beach. And he told them many things in parables, saying: "A sower went out to sow. And as he sowed, some seeds fell along the path, and the birds came and devoured them. Other seeds fell on rocky ground, where they had not much soil, and immediately they sprang up, since they had no depth of soil, but when the sun rose they were scorched; and since they had no root they withered away. Other seeds fell upon thorns, and the thorns grew up and choked them. Other seeds fell on good soil and brought forth grain, some a hundredfold, some sixty, some thirty. He who has ears, let him hear!"*

Jesus was saying, "Let him or her comprehend my meaning who is willing to." And I believe many did. Even if they got some of the details wrong in telling someone else, it didn't matter. They could still convey the main point: Christ wanted the seed, or word, He sowed to take root in them as in the good soil and to bear fruit.

But some were slow to understand. When His disciples asked why He spoke in parables, Jesus quoted the prophet Isaiah: "For this nation's heart has grown gross, fat and dull; their ears heavy and difficult of hearing, and their eyes they have tightly closed. But blessed—happy, fortunate and to be envied—are your eyes, because they do see, and your ears because they do hear" (Matthew 13:15-16). And then, as though to make sure, Jesus explains His parable in detail.

Now, I want you to reread Christ's parable and decide which of the following categories most typifies North American Christians:

One: "When anyone hears the word of the Kingdom," says Jesus, "And does not understand it, the evil one comes and snatches away what is sown in his heart; this is what was sown along the path."

Two: "As for what was sown on rocky ground, this is he who hears the word and immediately receives it with joy; yet he has no root in himself, but endures for a while, and when tribulation or persecution arises on account of the [kingdom] word, immediately he falls away."

Three: "As for what was sown among thorns, this is he who hears the word, but the cares of the world and the delights in riches choke the word, and it proves unfruitful." Mark reports it this way: "but the cares of the world and the delight in riches and the desire for other things, enter in and choke the word" (Mark 4:19). Or in Luke's version: "As for what fell among thorns, these are those who hear, but as they go on their way they are choked by the cares and riches and pleasures of life, and their fruit does not mature" (Luke 8:14).

Finally, category four: "As for what was sown on good soil, this is he who hears the word and understands it; he indeed bears fruit, and yields in one case a hundredfold, in another sixty and in another thirty."

If we were in a classroom, I could ask for hands as to which of these four categories most characterizes North American believers. I'm sure you've guessed by now that my leaning is toward category three—and I have a feeling that's what you would have said also. Isn't it interesting that having heard this parable nigh unto nausea, most believers still haven't come to grips with the basic fact that they are among those whose seed fell upon thorns, and the thorns have now grown up and choked them.

You know what I discovered long ago? I found I had to decide whether maturing in the Kingdom was important to me. Or would I choose to enjoy what most Americans consider their new inalienable rights—like reading a morning newspaper, relaxing with television in the evening, spending time buying pretty much whatever I wanted as long as I saved for it? What I discovered was that to pursue Kingdom secrets meant having to make certain choices. So for the last many years, we have lived without a TV set (you knew that already) and a daily paper. Why? Because I always seemed to have time for the paper and television, but not for Scripture and prayer and Kingdom pursuits. Without these things, which were personal "Thorns" for me, I was able to resolve my problem.

Your thorns may be different, but the bottom line is that the Kingdom must not be choked out by the cares, pleasures, interests, agenda of the world, whatever those are.

How grows your Kingdom seed, my friend?

When I think of how I long to nourish the Kingdom seed in my life, I think of one of the most beautiful of sights: a great field of standing grain. Those who have lived in the Great Plains states know what I mean. It represents so much work—farmers and God together in concert! So it is with spiritual harvests of thirty-, sixty-, and a hundredfold. It's a lot of work, but what a beautiful sight—and what a rich harvest!

Maybe, like some in the generation who heard Jesus in person, we hear but never understand; we see, but never perceive. According to Christ, if we can't grasp parables like this one, we can't go much further in our understanding. There is no sense digging for deeper Kingdom truths if we can't yet handle the obvious ones. Or as Jesus put it to His disciples in Matthew 13:11, "To you it has been given to know the secrets of the kingdom of heaven."

But read Christ's words in the next verse: "And to him who had, more will be given and he will have in abundance, but from him who has not, even what he has will be taken away." Luke 8:18 records the same thought, only in the form of a warning: "Take heed then how you hear; for to him who has will more be given and from him who has not, even what he thinks he has will be taken away." And in Luke 8:15—"So be among those who hear the word, hold it fast in an honest and good heart and bring forth fruit with patience."

---

*Kingdom secrets in abundance belong to hearers who hold fast to their truths and bear fruit.*

---

*The strange thing was, the more Hunter walked with the King, and the more the King talked about his plans, the more the boy could actually see what the King seemed to be seeing. Yes, here were sturdy houses being built. Hunter could hear the sound of children playing, running to catch balls and climbing on the equipment. He could actually see in his mind the bicycle races and the women and men gathering in the outdoor market with piles of fruit and containers of garden transplants. He could hear the music of the band in the band shell. He could imagine the gardens with everyone working in the soil, planting and hoeing and weeding and sharing the produce.*

*The city really was Bright City, no longer sad-looking, or dilapidated, or dangerous. It was under Restoration, with much to be done, certainly, but it was much better than it had seemed to the boy after the mudslinging riots. The King was near. The King had plans. The King could see the end of Restoration. Hunter heard the watch cry, "The Kingdom comes!" And the sound of the repeated echo thrilled his heart once again. "Yes," he reminded himself. "The Kingdom comes!"*

**From the *Tales of the Restoration* story:**
**"Taxi-lore"**

CHAPTER 21

# SMALL-TOWN THINKERS

~

S OME SAY SMALL TOWNS and small thinking go together. Having
been raised in a small community, such a statement makes me defensive.
I look back on those years as some of the finest any boy could have wanted.

But before coming to the *Chapel of the Air* broadcast, I also pastored
twelve years in the heart of Chicago, then the second-largest city in America.
So I've seen the good and the bad of city life as well. From that experience, I
discovered a big city forces you to think expansively. Whether good or bad,
it's almost a given. In a rural setting, by contrast, one has the privilege of
being more provincial.

I make this point to underscore something quite interesting as we study
Christ's message of the Kingdom. If Jesus had wanted a group of men who
could think big—big enough to consider changing the world—why gather
His disciples from Galilee? People from there were thought of as country
bumpkins! You could hear when Galileans were coming—by their accents!

From the beginning why didn't Christ look more for the "Saul of Tarsus"
type? With a big-city background, educated, culturally attuned—he was a
man who traveled and knew how to get things done. You would think a
king would choose someone who understood power structures. But not
Galilean fishermen!

Let me stress again that Jesus did have visions of changing the world.
"For God so loved the world that he gave his only begotten Son." He said,
"Go into all the world and preach the gospel to the whole creation." "You
shall be my witnesses to the end of the earth." Maybe you recall the picture
in Revelation 7 of the "great multitude which no man could number, from
every nation, from all tribes and peoples and tongues, standing before the
throne, and before the lamb clothed in white robes."

For that matter, when Christ chose the word kingdom to introduce what He was talking about, the whole scheme had a certain sense of grandness to begin with. Suppose you are in a small town and talk to others about joining you in a business venture. You just might succeed. But try rallying the town's support for a worldwide kingdom! You may find people wanting to throw you off the nearest cliff just like they attempted to do to Jesus when He shared His thoughts in His home town of Nazareth.

But Jesus would not change what He had His mind and heart set on. Christ thought big! Let's focus on this size factor as we examine another of Christ's Kingdom parables found in Matthew, Mark and Luke. Its basic point concerns the growth of His following.

In Matthew it reads, "The kingdom of heaven [Mark and Luke say 'kingdom of God'—again note how these terms are used interchangeably] is like a grain of mustard seed."

Most Bible scholars feel Christ was referring to the black mustard plant, which has a thick main stem and grows as high as ten feet with branches strong enough to bear the weight of a bird. Even so, the seeds are like nothing. In Israel I've held such mustard seeds in my hand. You can hardly see them. They're minute—almost like ground pepper.

So when Jesus said the kingdom of heaven is like a grain of mustard seed, in the minds of His early followers that initial statement was quite realistic in terms of what they felt about themselves. They were small. But Christ continued, "The kingdom of heaven is like a grain of mustard seed which a man took and sowed in his field; it is the smallest of all seeds, but when it has grown it is the greatest of shrubs and becomes a tree, so that the birds of the air come and make nests in its branches."

Now, a parable is not an allegory. In other words, with a parable like this you don't have to figure out what each element represents. We aren't to waste time on whether the birds or the man who sowed the seed symbolize something. Parables have one basic point, which is why Christ used them so frequently—so people could understand them, remember them, and be able to tell them to others as well. And this Kingdom parable of the mustard seed explained to Christ's hearers that what's beginning as something extremely small is going to be surprising in terms of how big it gets.

What's more strange is that this message (which at the time probably smacked of exaggeration) is now such an understatement, it doesn't even begin to describe what has transpired through the years. Partly that's because

Christ's disciples chose to overcome their smallness and to identify with what their leader believed. "If we're going to follow Him," they apparently reasoned, "We're just going to have to learn to be small-town people with big-world ideas!"

And they made the transition. They even broke out of their Jewish inclusiveness and went out to plant the Kingdom flag everywhere—even in the teeth of enemy opposition! I feel like clapping for them!

I wonder, with the incredible modern resources at our command, if we can identify that closely with the King's desires. Or are we more interested in the personal advantages of Kingdom involvement? We think far less about the Kingdom's growth and greatness and with where our King is in His thoughts. Maybe we are the new generation of Galileans who need changing!

---

*To identify with our King,*
*we must work at developing a worldview.*

---

We can't afford to think only in terms of our desires, our friends, our surroundings, our comforts. To identify with our unique King, we must develop a world perspective because "God was in Christ reconciling the world to himself." Jesus said, "I am the light of the world." "Behold the lamb of God," preached John the Baptist, "Who takes away the sin of the world!" The Samaritans had it right in John 4:42 when they said, "We know that this is indeed the Savior of the world!"

What about you? Do you have to fight the tendency to be concerned only about your part of it? Let me ask you the same question in other ways that make it easier for you to formulate a quick response. Is there a missionary or two with whom you keep in close touch, working as a backup person to service their needs in another part of the world? And are you current with what's going on in their service? Have you purposely developed an interest in one or two given mission fields, becoming well-informed about the overall Kingdom advance there? India, Bolivia, France, New Guinea, Mexico, Ivory Coast, Nepal?

"Nepal?" you say. "You mean there are people trying to witness for Christ in that wild mountainous nation? Why, I've heard that Nepali law forbids any proselytizing!"

It does. But Nepal is one of the places represented by the growth of that tiny Kingdom mustard seed. Our King had Nepal in mind as a place of Kingdom expansion even as He did America. And I'm of the opinion that some of us need to make Nepal our own.

All of us have to start small—pick one missionary, one country—and learn to reduce the colossal to a manageable size. Because we can't know every mission organization or every missionary doesn't mean we can't become experts regarding one or two. No apostle won the world alone. Each set out in different directions, but together they did so much. And so must we as we learn to see a world beyond just our own.

Certainly there are enough believers in North America to spread the task among many. The question is not are you doing everything you can—but are you doing something—something that shows the expansion of the Kingdom is as close to your heart as it is to your King's? You see, Kingdom people think bigger than most—it's characteristic of them!

"David," a man wrote to me, "I've finally figured out what it is I don't like about your ministry. You're always pushing—never satisfied—it doesn't matter what I do, tomorrow you'll have something new. Let up, will you!"

If he expresses your thoughts, let me clear something up. What I've shared in this chapter is not my thinking.

I'm only giving what I feel to be an accurate reflection of the thinking of God's anointed King. To associate with Him, I believe, we—you and I—have to work at developing a bigger worldview!

If that seems tough, consider again how heavy such a task must have appeared to our first-century brothers and sisters. From their example, we can conclude: Look out when small-town Kingdom people get big-world ideas!

~

*Strangely, the more the little girl used her loud voice inside when she was supposed to, the less she used her outside voice inside when she wasn't supposed to. She did not know that this training would serve her well, when in years to come the King would ask her to use her powerful outside voice to preach in the streets of distant cities about his Kingdom, and her quiet inside voice to speak quietly and in private with those who felt different, all alone, or in need of an understanding friend.*

**From the *Tales of the Restoration* story:**
**"The Girl With the Very Loud Outside Voice"**

# CHAPTER 22

# KING AND JUDGE

❦

I T MUST BE FRIGHTENING to be put on trial. Courtrooms are not the friendliest of places. I mention this because there is a Kingdom parable that's much like a courtroom scene—the great judgment at the close of the age. Matthew 13:24-25 is where this parable begins. Christ told His followers, "The kingdom of heaven may be compared to a man who sowed good seed in his field; but while men were sleeping, his enemy sowed weeds among the wheat, and went away."

If someone actually did that to you, sowed weeds among your wheat, how would you feel? I think it would make you pretty mad!

Christ continued,

> So when the plants came up and bore grain, then the weeds appeared also. And the servants of the householder came and said to him, "Sir, did you not sow good seed in your field? How then has it weeds?" He said to them, "An enemy has done this."
>
> The servants said to him, "Then do you want us to go and gather them?" But he said, "No, lest in gathering the weeds you root up the wheat along with them. Let both grow together until the harvest, and at harvest time I will tell the reapers, 'Gather the weeds first and bind them in bundles to be burned, but gather the wheat into my barn.'"

Now if you're having trouble understanding this, verse 36 may be comforting. Christ's disciples weren't sure they knew what He was saying either. "Explain to us the parable of the weeds of the field," they said.

Jesus shared that the field was the world, the good seeds were the sons of the Kingdom, and the weeds the sons of the evil one, or the devil.

The reapers were angels, and the harvest represents the close of the age. Then in Matthew 13:40-42, He continues, "Just as the weeds are gathered and burned with fire, so will it be at the close of the age. The Son of Man will send his angels, and they will gather out of his kingdom all causes of sin and all evildoers, and throw them into the furnace of fire; there men will weep and gnash their teeth."

That's frightening, isn't it! Bundling up men like weeds and tossing them into the fire! "Then the righteous"—note that word—"The righteous will shine like the sun in the kingdom of their Father. He who has ears, let him hear." That is, pay attention to what's being said!

So at the same time Christ is recruiting members for His Kingdom, He's also warning everyone there will be an awful judgment of those who choose to give their allegiance to the enemy. In Matthew 13:47-50, this truth is reemphasized. "Again," says Christ, "The kingdom of heaven is like a net which was thrown into the sea and gathered fish of every kind; when it was full, men drew it ashore and sat down and sorted the good into vessels but threw away the bad. So it will be at the close of the age. The angels will come out and separate the evil from the righteous and throw them [the evil ones] into the furnace of fire; there men will weep and gnash their teeth."

Now I can just hear someone saying, "Well praise the Lord! I'm okay on this parable anyway. I mean, these Kingdom parables have been really getting to me. Not that I don't feel badly about people getting tossed into hell, but at least I do know I'm a part of Christ's Kingdom. I'm saved and that's settled."

"Good," I respond, "because it's only the righteous who escape the judgment of the great King!"

"What?" you question.

I said:

---

*Only the righteous escape
the awful judgment of the great King.*

---

I purposely used the word righteous because it appears in both of these judgment parables—"The righteous will shine like the sun," and "The angels will come out and separate the evil from the righteous." It is also in Matthew 25, where it mentions the King coming in His glory and all the angels with Him. Do you remember how the question is asked by the righteous? "Lord, when did we see thee hungry and feed thee?" This long Kingdom passage ends with the King saying to those on His left, "Depart from me, you cursed, into the eternal fire prepared for the devil and his angels. For I was hungry and you gave me no food. ... As you did it not to one of the least of these you did it not to me. And they will go away into eternal punishment, but the righteous unto eternal life."

Do you know what the Bible means by the word righteous? Actually, the way it is used in Scripture is quite involved. My Bible dictionary devotes fourteen full pages to explaining righteousness as it appears in the Old and New Testaments. But for the moment, let us excuse the Bible scholars and try to pinpoint a working definition.

I always connect righteousness with rightness, doing what is right before God and in relation to others. It's like Christ always doing the will of the Father and always being upright in His dealings with others. Making God and others the focus of our rightness helps us avoid self-righteousness—the opposite of what's being advocated. Self-righteousness makes sure others notice us. But it is pretentious, like the Pharisees about whom Christ said, "Don't practice your piety before men like they do in order to be seen by them."

Righteousness is rightness—doing what is right and pleasing to God and in regard to others.

"Just a minute," cautions someone. "It sounds like you're implying that we escape judgment by doing what is right."

No.

Paul writes in Romans how the Gentiles, who did not pursue righteousness, have attained it; that is, they achieved their righteousness through faith. But Israel, who pursued the righteousness that is based on law (or works), did not succeed (Romans 9:30-32).

But is Paul arguing that we can just do as we please because works are not the issue?

Not at all.

We are to "Walk in newness of life, yielding our members to God as instruments of righteousness." "You have died to the law ... so that you may belong to another, to him who has been raised from the dead in order that you may bear fruit for God" (Romans 7:4).

Bearing fruit for God leads me back to one last Kingdom passage (Matthew 7:17-23) from Christ's lips concerning the final judgment: "Every sound tree bears good fruit, but the bad tree bears evil fruit. A sound tree cannot bear evil fruit, nor can a bad tree bear good fruit. Every tree that does not bear good fruit is cut down and thrown into the fire."

Then comes this sobering paragraph: "Not everyone who says to me, 'Lord, Lord' shall enter the kingdom of heaven, but he who does the will of my Father who is in heaven [or he who is truly righteous—not just in talk, but in deed]."

"On that day many [it doesn't read 'a couple'—it says 'many'] will say to me, 'Lord, Lord, did we not prophesy in your name, and do many mighty works in your name?'"

Christ, God's anointed King and Judge, says, "Then will I declare to them, 'I never knew you; depart from me, you evildoers.'" He doesn't say, "I once knew you, but not anymore." He says, "I *never* knew you, depart from me. You have never been among the righteous. You are evildoers. Only the righteous—those truly clothed in the fashion of their King—escape this awful judgment." Or in Christ's words in verse 20: "One can tell whose righteousness is mine and whose isn't by the fruit that's born."

What am I trying to convey?

I want to make sure you are among the righteous who escape judgment. Therefore, I don't want you to presume upon God, to assume Christ's righteousness if most of the signs say otherwise.

It's interesting to me that during times of great revival—when God's truths come alive in all the burning realities of eternity—that many of the converts are people who have been in the Church for years.

Thank God for such times of genuine revival. Otherwise, what a frightful experience it would be for some church people to stand trial before Him and hear pronounced, "No, I never knew you!"

~

And inside the King continued to speak the children's names, and with each naming the Orphan Keeper grew grayer, more haggard, leaking hot air. Her hair lost its luster, her teeth grew black and straggly until all could see her for her true self: a wicked hag who had gorged on the energy and youth and beauty of the children given to her keeping, a faker whose evil power was not her own, a no-people in disguise, as were all who gave themselves to do the will of the Enchanter. Finally she was nothing but a pile of dust covered by filthy red and purple rags, her gold melted and her jewels turned to dust.

**From the *Tales of the Resistance* story:**
**"The Orphan Exodus"**

CHAPTER 23

# Pluck It Out

~

IT'S FRUSTRATING! As a radio preacher I can't see how people respond to what I say. If someone goes to sleep while I'm preaching in a church, it annoys me! I want to go over and wake that person up. Listeners whose minds are elsewhere is a common problem preachers face.

But I have a feeling Jesus never had any trouble keeping people's attention with His Kingdom talk. Not only did He effectively use parables, He said things that made it practically impossible for his hearers to not stay alert. For example, "You have heard that it was said, 'You shall not commit adultery.' But I say to you that everyone who looks at a woman lustfully has already committed adultery with her in his heart!"

Suddenly everybody in the audience is listening with both ears. Even today a dull preacher can temporarily startle a chronic sanctuary-sleeper by mentioning sex every so often.

But now hear Christ's next words. "If your right eye causes you to sin, pluck it out and throw it away. And if your right hand causes you to sin, cut it off and throw it away, for it is better that you lose one of your members than that your whole body go into hell."

Pretty strong talk! Did Jesus actually want those considering Kingdom involvement to go through life handless and sightless? The answer is obviously no. But He did want His hearers to understand that eternity apart from the love of God was a staggering price to pay for the fleeting pleasures afforded by sin. The devil has some fancy lures, and every one of them has a hook in it. He's a master at landing his victims in his boat of the damned.

Now this sermon of Christ's came early in His ministry. Clear lines about who was a disciple and who wasn't were just beginning to be understood. The message of the cross and the idea of being born anew of God's Spirit to enter the Kingdom had not yet been shared. Jesus basically spoke to Jewish listeners who by their presence indicated their desire to hear a word from God. And what He said to people living under the law is that it is better to take drastic action to avoid sin than to be condemned forever to hell.

Well aware that I can't just erase the difference in time and audience from that setting to ours, I still feel Christ's words have current value. In today's world, would you not agree that men and women, even believers, need to be reminded that God and sin don't go together? "This is the message we have heard from him," wrote John, "That God is light and in him is no darkness at all. If we say we have fellowship with him while we walk in darkness we lie and do not live according to the truth."

Isn't it also appropriate for contemporary mankind to be warned that God will condemn people to hell because of sin? No less than Peter wrote, "For if God did not spare the angels when they sinned, but cast them into hell, then the Lord knows how to keep the unrighteous under punishment until the day of judgment, and especially those who indulge in the lust of defiling passion and despise authority."

If I am to represent Christ's thought, it seems only right to go further and state that as a basic principle, sin should be avoided like the plague. And how that warning needs to be sounded today! But can my sophisticated contemporaries hear it without reacting? Fire alarms and tornado sirens are received with gratitude. But if a minister raises his voice regarding the terrible destruction brought about in lives by sin, too often he's considered a fanatic—even though he carries the heartbreak of seeing this truth proven again and again. If a doctor speaks out against the misuse of drugs, he's an expert. Let a member of the clergy take the same stand on moral and biblical grounds, and people ask, "Who does he think he is, making judgments about right and wrong?"

But is that not what prophetic ministry is all about? We serve society by sharing the mind of the King on such matters. And I know God desires all people be warned to stay away from sin. Paul wrote in Romans, "The wages of sin is death"; and in Corinthians, "Come to your right mind and sin no more."

Maybe it's time to hear again Christ's words about especially difficult sins that require extreme action: "If your right eye causes you to sin, pluck it out and throw it away; it is better that you lose one of your members than that your whole body be thrown into hell!"

What Jesus said is literally true. To be without an eye now is less fearful than to be forever outside the scope of God's love in the world to come. I don't think His desire was that everyone with a problem of lust pluck out an eyeball from its socket like a ripe grape. And I doubt if any of His hearers heard His words that way. They knew it was Christ's manner of emphasizing His point. What they probably heard Him saying was:

*Damning sins require drastic action.*

If you are one who because of a certain pet sin is being kept apart from God, then maybe a voice beyond mine is confronting you right now saying, "The path you're traveling is very dangerous; you need to make a radical change and soon!"

What is your sin? Perhaps it is the problem about which Christ spoke. For years you have toyed with lust and now it has you bound foot and hand. Will you vow before God to never again look at a magazine or book or film that feeds the sexual appetite in a way contrary to the beautiful plan for men and women established in Scripture? That's right, for you that may be radical—but so is hell!

Maybe you never had a problem with alcohol before—but now things have changed. Why then do you refuse to deal with what everyone else affirms is out of control? Inside, don't you know that unless you make a significant counter-move soon, your whole life may fall apart because of drink? Pluck it out. Ask others for help if need be, or visit an AA meeting.

Or maybe it's peer pressure: "But my friends will tease me if I'm not up on the most popular songs." It's very likely you're right. But can you afford to continue paying the price of mental purity often required by this habit? You see, life is made up of choices, and as you mature you'll find that even Kingdom members tend to make some pretty stupid ones!

Some of you need to break off a friendship and you know it. It's dragging you down further and further. As painful as it sounds to take such action, it's less awesome than saying goodbye to God. So settle the issue right now and make your move. The Lord will honor your faith.

Well, I can't name every sin that might have you in its grip—self-pity, homosexuality, gossip, worry, jealousy, greed—but I can suggest that when you are bound there are still mature Kingdom members who can help if you will take the first step and go to them.

I remember one of the stories I used to read to my children. It is called *The Great Surprise*. It tells the true account of a man who made his fortune by cheating others. He had sold his soul for money, and for him to break that hold would be next to impossible. But confronted by this same Jesus, Zacchaeus sensed that for him change was now or never. In Scripture this story is found in Luke 19. It occurs as Christ is on His way to Jerusalem for the final time. Because it is so well-known, let me share it the way the children's book tells it. Zacchaeus said to Christ:

> *"I don't think of anyone but me!*
> *The extra money that I take, it's very plain to see,*
> *Makes others poor, and here I sit as wealthy as a king!*
> *Before another day goes by, I'll do an honest thing.*
> *My clothes and food and all I own I shall divide in two.*
> *I'll take half to the poorer folk, and … I know what I'll do!*
> *What I owe to any man I'll multiply by four.*
> *I'll start to pay my debts today, and I will cheat no more!"*
> *His children shouted out: "Hurrah! I'll share some toys of mine."*
> *His wife and servants also cheered: "We think that sounds just fine!"*
> *When Jesus rose to leave, he said, "I've had a splendid stay!*
> *Zacchaeus, it does give Me joy to know you feel this way.*
> *And you will find that this has been a very special day!"*

Then the last page has no writing—just a picture. People are standing around dumbfounded because the little man in the middle of the page is handing out money. But on his face is this huge smile.

Zacchaeus had turned a comer—now what about you?

~

Amanda wept as she looked up at the King. "I thought you would never want to see me again."

The King wiped her tears, but she wept all the more. All her sorrows tumbled out: "I disobeyed. I lied. I cursed Caretaker in my heart. I loved a forbidden thing. I brought fire into Great Park. Everyone has suffered because of me. Send me away. I don't deserve kingslove."

The King folded the weeping child into his arms. "Don't leave me, Amanda," he whispered. "We've all been so lonely without you."

**From the *Tales of the Kingdom* story:**
**"Trial by Fire"**

CHAPTER 24

# THE SERVANT MINDSET

⁓

STUDIES INDICATE that children from wealthy and privileged families tend to lose their natural sensitivity. Questions like "Daddy, how come those people are so poor?" are often met with the standard answer, "They're lazy" or "That's just the way some people choose to live." The child soon learns that certain questions are best not asked and that it's wise "not to associate with people unlike us!"

Even people raised with little who then experience worldly success all too frequently forget the pain of their earlier poverty. Ever so subtly the process sets in: as they enjoy the new comforts of life, they distance themselves from those in lower economic brackets.

Historically, and certainly in Bible times, this distancing from the poor has been especially true of royalty—except for the King we've been studying. Never did He allow His popularity or rank to isolate Him from the problems of the powerless. Rather than becoming more and more exclusive when proclaiming His Kingdom, He declared, "You who are poor, what ruler had ever before been truly concerned about you? But now you are blessed with my announcement of the kingdom of God. Those who weep, blessed are you for at last you shall find comfort and joy…" and so on.

Christ's ongoing ministry further underscored this concern for the lowly. Those to whom He reached out were often the offscouring of the earth. What other leader took notice when a man full of leprosy cried out, "Unclean"? Or when a wild, naked, demon-possessed wretch came screaming out of the graveyard? Or when a self-conscious woman suffering for years from an issue of blood tugged at His robe?

This emphasis came out in His teaching as well. "When you give a dinner," Jesus said, "don't invite your friends or relatives or rich neighbors lest they also invite you in return and you be repaid. But when you give a feast invite the poor, the maimed, the lame, the blind, and you will be blessed because they can't repay you."

Do you realize how wonderfully different this King was when compared to most others recorded in history?

Shortly before Christ's triumphal entry into Jerusalem, this incident occurred: "Then the mother of James and John came up to him and kneeling before him asked, 'Command that these two sons of mine may sit one on your right hand and one on your left in your kingdom'" (Matthew 20). Here's a Jewish mother doing a little timely politicizing!

When the ten heard it, they were indignant at the two brothers. But Jesus called them to Him and said, "You know that the rulers of the Gentiles lord it over them. It shall not be so among you, but whoever would be great among you must be your servant, and whoever would be first among you must be your slave."

With this statement Jesus contradicted what everyone had always accepted as fact: that leaders have a right to lord it over others and great men should expect the positions of honor. "No, my kingdom is the exception!" said Christ. "But the exception is the way it was meant to be all along. Now I personally have reset the standard. The Son of Man has come not to be served, but to serve."

Again, do you realize how unusual Christ was in this regard? Picture Him in today's setting and you'll see what I mean. If you accept the gospel records regarding His healing gifts, His miracles and His skills as a communicator, as a single male in his early thirties alive in our culture today Christ would easily be the most sought-out personality in the nation.

Doing no more than He did when He was here, I am sure Jesus would draw crowds beyond anyone's imagination. If the feeding of the five thousand were covered via satellite, He would become an awesome world figure. Say *60 Minutes* devoted a program to Him; I wonder how they would present this Jesus of Nazareth who some claim to be the Messiah? Impressive ... free from scandal ... opinionated ... idealistic ... somewhat mysterious ... to a certain degree, an enigma ... an obvious leader, yet one who doesn't understand the accoutrements of power ... so wise and still so naïve in the ways of the world. Will this be considered a fatal flaw? That possibly he takes too seriously what the prophets wrote about the Christ being a suffering servant!

Did you pick up as well that this King expected His subjects to behave in the same manner as He did? Just to underscore the point, in the evening before the day He knew He was to die—without question a time everyone would excuse a monarch for being a bit self-centered—even then John records the following:

> When Jesus knew that his hour had come to depart out of this world to his Father, he rose, laid aside his garments, and girded himself with a towel. Then he poured water into a basin and began to wash his disciples feet.
> "Do you know what I have done to you?" he asked. "You call me teacher and Lord; and you are right, for so I am. If then, your lord and teacher has washed your feet, you also ought to wash one another's feet. For I have given you an example, that you also should do as I have done to you. Truly, truly, I say to you, a servant is not greater than his master. If you know these things, blessed are you if you do them!"

*To be great in God's Kingdom, assume the mindset of a servant.*

Turned around it would read this way: To be small in God's Kingdom, look out for old number-one: yourself.

This concept is so hard for us to process in this day. It is totally out-of-sync with what our society says.

Just a caution, this certainly isn't the servant stereotype Americans sometimes picture. By servant, Christ didn't mean someone who's learned it's always best to say, "Yes, sir; whatever you say, sir!"—always living in the shadow of important people. Christ wasn't that way at all. He was extremely self-assured, confrontational, issuing orders, calling others to follow Him. So being the kind of servant He has in mind doesn't mean we stop looking people in the eye when we speak, or lose all initiative, or take on only menial tasks. Not at all!

Rather, a servant mindset means we force ourselves to stop thinking it's the obligation of others to serve us, and purposely consider how we can serve them, especially those who are less advantaged. Their needs, their desires, their dreams, must be as important as ours.

Here then is a unique Kingdom quality—leaders who truly know how to serve. When this is lost, something beautiful has been taken from us. If the pampered, the proud and the privileged regain all the places of honor in Christ's Kingdom, then it's just like any other.

If you agree with this concept of servanthood as modeled by Christ, let me suggest some practical ways to implement it. Rather than attempting to resolve this matter through one gigantic effort, I'd recommend you begin slowly. Ask the Lord to give you direction today regarding just one person you can effectively serve on Christ's behalf. Think of how you can be of help to that person through whatever special resources you have been blessed with.

Caution. Don't jump into doing God's work without first asking Him for help. Needs are abundant, and you'll not be able to meet them all. That's why you must learn to pray something like the following:

Father, I know I can't learn about a servant mindset on my own. After all, I'm not yet very adept at it! During the next twenty-four hours would you make me aware of a service I can perform that normally I wouldn't even notice? Prompt me please to pay attention at such a time, and I'll do my best to be obedient to what you have in mind. Amen.

If you pray regularly like this, soon the very difficult injunction from our Lord about Kingdom humility will become more natural to you. And when you become adept at this prayer, I predict you'll also begin to think that one of the reasons the Kingdom has not advanced further than it has is because we have all but forfeited the attractiveness of our great King's role reversal.

Can you imagine what it would be like if all Kingdom people treasured the return of the servant mindset? Oh, that the servant ways of our King will again be revealed in the lives of His subjects!

*It was the King, the King who had endured Burning Place to lift the enchantment that had held this city in the Enchanter's power. Little Child had never seen him as now, disguised as a common streetsweeper, hands callused from hard work, face filthy from flung dirt, pain shadowing his eyes. It was the King now cleaning up the mud the people of his Kingdom had been slinging at one another. It was the King, suffering silently the blows of dirt that fell on him. It was the King with a wound on his cheek.*

**From the *Tales of the Restoration* story:**
**"Mudslinging"**

# CHAPTER 25

# THE WILL OF THE KING

◿

IN ANCIENT TIMES a king's word was law. Today, when our elected officials are held more accountable for their actions, I'm not sure we can begin to appreciate the absolute power of an old-time monarch. A thousand years ago, when a king spoke, people trembled. Subjects didn't say, "I'll, ah … take that into consideration, your majesty." What they replied was, "Yes, your majesty!"

The closest modern equivalent I can think of would be a decision handed down by the Supreme Court. You wouldn't argue with it; you would just accept it.

In the New Testament, just a word from King Herod was enough to slaughter all the male children in Bethlehem two years old and younger. A king like Herod might be hated, but because of his title and power he was still treated with great respect.

We have been concentrating on Christ's message of the Kingdom of God. But to use the word kingdom presupposes a king. The crowds that surrounded Him at His triumphal entry into Jerusalem were right in assuming this, even though they didn't understand Christ was out to depose a greater enemy than Herod or Caesar. They were right on the money when they understood Jesus of Nazareth to be more than just another itinerate preacher.

Nor were the Romans who occupied the country unaware of what was in the making. Pilate's question to Christ at His trial was not without foundation: "Are you the king of the Jews?"

We'll look at the Roman response to the Kingdom in the chapter "A Case of Expediency." Right now I'm more concerned about the reaction of the Jewish religious powers to Christ's kingship or Kingdom. They're the ones who prompted Pilate's question by shouting, "We found this man perverting our nation, forbidding us to give tribute to Caesar and saying that he himself is Christ, a king."

Whether or not Christ was God's anointed King was so important a matter that the chief priests pleaded with Pilate, "Don't write over the cross The King of the Jews, but that this man said, I am King of the Jews."

Even at the crucifixion they jeered and shouted, "Let the king of Israel, the Christ, come down from the cross, that we may see and believe."

Who were these people, and why did they so strongly oppose Christ and His Kingdom? Well, there were two main Jewish religious parties—the Sadducees and the Pharisees. Both wanted to do away with Jesus, but for different reasons.

We would tend to view the religious interests of the Sadducees as political in nature, almost the way present evangelicals view old-time religious liberals. From Acts we learn the Sadducees did not believe in angels, spirits, or resurrection. So the supernatural was hardly paramount in their thinking. But the here-and-now not only had to be dealt with, it was of vital concern to them. The Sadducees were comprised of the old aristocratic, monied families of Jerusalem who understood survival, compromise and power. They didn't like Rome, but politically they had learned to live with it. Because in spite of the fact that they were Jews under foreign domination, they had still carved out for themselves rather comfortable lives.

So a young Galilean who drew crowds and talked of a new kingdom but appeared to know little or nothing about power structures was a definite threat to their position. Not only did he make them nervous because he challenged the status quo ("He stirs up the people" was their precise comment), during passion week he had the audacity to interfere with their lucrative temple concessions and then quite openly accused them of knowing neither the Scriptures nor the power of God.

By way of contrast, the Pharisees had the hearts of the people—before Christ, anyway. Not elitist like the Sadducees, they were what people might think of today as religious fanatics—unfortunately, to a fault. At best they were legalists, arguing endlessly over the fine points of the law, but hopelessly missing the spirit behind it. At worst, well, Christ called them hypocrites.

To see these two groups in action, read Matthew 21-23. Even with this little background I think you'll be able to sort out what's happening. When reading the phrase "chief priests and Pharisees," see it as "Sadducees and Pharisees," because the chief priests were Sadducees.

The final of the three chapters—Matthew 23—shows Jesus repeatedly criticizing the Pharisees and scribes. The scribes were the educated authorities on the law. We might call them scholars—mostly Pharisees, but a few Sadducees too. A scribe would be like a noted Bible scholar, about whom, without more information, you're not sure if he's liberal or conservative.

In this chapter Christ says, "The scribes [or scholars of the law] and Pharisees [the legalists] sit on Moses' seat; so practice and observe whatever they tell you, but not what they do; for they preach but do not practice. They bind heavy burdens, hard to bear, and lay them on men's shoulders, but they themselves will not move them with their fingers."

If the basic feeling of the Sadducees was that Christ's Kingdom preaching was rocking the boat, the Pharisees thought it invalid because the Kingdom simply didn't fit their grid. Christ had been clearly told by them what the Pharisees agreed upon was supposedly the truth of God and the universe! Since Jesus hadn't adjusted accordingly, he and his kingdom must now be exposed as fraudulent!

What neither the Pharisees or Sadducees realized was that Jesus was a true king—He was indeed the Christ, God's anointed King, the Messiah. No greater or more powerful king had ever walked this earth. And because of their response, He was taking the Kingdom of God away from them and giving it to a nation producing the fruits of it (Matthew 25:43). Think of it!

Kings with authority don't have to negotiate. They're especially not going to negotiate non-negotiables. Even the religious world couldn't expect to alter the terms of God's anointed King.

Allow me to repeat this idea slightly differently for my key sentence for this chapter.

*The religious world is rightly expected
to accept the terms of God's anointed King.*

I wonder if in the present North American religious world we ever attempt to argue with the great King's word? "Your majesty, there's tremendous pressure from society to stay relevant. I feel we have to make certain concessions regarding kingdom entry requirements."

Christ's answer: "Do not be deceived—neither the immoral, nor adulterers, nor sexual perverts, nor thieves, nor the greedy, nor drunkards will inherit the kingdom of God."

"Jesus, I've told the people how great you are, and that to follow you is to expect to live like a king."

Scripture reads, "You are made worthy of the kingdom through suffering. But God will repay with affliction those who afflict you, and grant rest to you when your Lord is revealed from heaven."

"Why even question it, your majesty? At church conferences prominent people have always been given the places of honor as we are doing."

Jesus replies, "Whoever humbles himself as a child, he is the greatest in the kingdom."

"Ah, careful what you say to the new generation, my Lord. The focus today is freedom. Dos and don'ts went out with the advent of television."

He answers, "I will say to them, unless their righteousness exceeds that of the Pharisees, they will never enter the kingdom of God."

"Careful, my sovereign, with this challenge to your Kingdom members to pick up the slack from government cutbacks in social services. The subjects are not taking to it well!"

Christ replies, "How do they expect then to inherit the Kingdom prepared for them if when I was hungry they gave me no food—naked and they did not clothe me?"

"Good teacher, I feel it's important to let you know that your Kingdom only fits our doctrinal system as a future hope. We see it as having little immediate bearing on us."

The Messiah: "The Kingdom is not coming with signs to be observed. Behold, the kingdom of God is in the midst of you."

"My sovereign, I know the people well. They will only take so much spiritual stretching, my Lord; then they will shut us all off."

Jesus declares, "Not everyone who says to me, 'Lord, Lord,' shall enter the kingdom of heaven, but he who does the will of my Father who is in heaven. On that day many will say to me, 'Lord, Lord, did we not prophesy in your name, and cast out demons in your name, and do many mighty works in your name? And then will I declare to them, I never knew you; depart from me you evildoers.'"

Well, there you see it. As I said before, negotiating with old-time, strong-willed monarchs can be thankless work. Maybe it's still true. The religious world is rightly expected to accept the terms of God's anointed King!

~

*Children know they are forbidden to keep dragon eggs, because a dragonet soon hatches from the egg and achieves full growth six months later. The baby dragon's scales harden. It begins to breathe fire. At first, there are short blasts of warm air, then later great searing torches of flame. The dragon has become cunning and cannot be trusted. So a sign on the shores of Lake Marmo reads: "It Is Forbidden to Keep Dragon Eggs."*

*The two eggs Princess Amanda found one day many months after Hero's arrival were bronze. They glowed like amber jewels in the sunlight. Perhaps she meant to carry them to Caretaker. Perhaps she thought that they were old and shriveled inside. Perhaps she forgot. But she did not take them to Caretaker's Cottage.*

**From the *Tales of the Kingdom* story:**
**"Princess Amanda and the Dragon"**

# CHAPTER 26

# ONE REQUEST

~

SOMEONE WANTS YOU to do him a favor. Would you be willing to? Your answer will probably depend on what it is he wants, but I'll fill you in on that later. First let me tell you who's making the request: a king.

"A king?" you say. "A real live monarch?"

That's right. The greatest king of them all.

"What's his name?"

Jesus.

"Oh, Jesus, sure! But didn't He turn that position down when people attempted to make Him their ruler?"

True. He refused to be king on their terms, but He is a king nevertheless. Throughout His ministry He talked often of His Kingdom, which would be meaningless if He weren't a king.

Witnesses at His trial accused him this way: "We found this man forbidding us to give tribute to Caesar, and saying that he himself is Christ the King."

To complete the picture, we can read in Revelation: "Then I saw heaven opened, and behold, a white horse! He who sat upon it is called Faithful and True. On his robe and on his thigh he has a name inscribed, King of Kings, and Lord of Lords!"

So He's a king, all right!

Now about the favor that he is asking. It was voiced the evening of the final day before His awful crucifixion. Let's bring the scene to mind.

All week the atmosphere in Jerusalem had been tense. The city, jammed with pilgrims arriving for Passover, had witnessed an intense conflict between Christ and the established religious leaders appointed to office by the Romans. It began when Jesus, in the manner of a king, rode into the city amid the shouts of the crowds. Sitting on a donkey, He came in peace. (Astride a horse, as in the Revelation passage, His arrival would have signified Him coming prepared for battle.)

The controversy heated up when Christ threw the dove-sellers and money-changers out of the temple, temporarily disrupting a lucrative business of the powerful Jewish house of Annas. Charges and countercharges were exchanged in the temple as He taught, until finally it was no longer a question of "If" but "When" the Sadducees would make a move to have Him silenced. In that case, would Jesus ask the common folk to take up arms?

Christ, knowing that armed conflict was not His Father's will, waited for another option to unfold—to sacrifice Himself for the sins of the people. Those words are easy to say, of course, unless you're the one who must face the agony of Roman crucifixion.

"One of you will betray me," Jesus said with deep sadness, talking to men with whom He had lived for three years. "It would have been better for that man if he had not been born." But the strong warning was not enough to stop Judas from slipping out, to keep the traitorous appointment he had made.

With the restraint of the betrayer removed, Christ now said, "I have earnestly desired to eat this Passover with you before I suffer" (Luke 22:15). But that He must soon suffer hadn't seemed to register sufficiently with the remaining eleven. Taken up with all the Kingdom talk of the week, they now were wrangling over who should be regarded as the greatest among them.

Often Jewish prophets resorted to what we call object lessons when it seemed their message was not getting across. For Jesus, this was one of those times. Possibly His apostles were overconfident. When it came to power, had they not seen their Master quiet the raging storm with a word? Did He not feed five thousand with almost nothing? Weren't the demons subject to Him? Hadn't He most recently even raised the dead? And didn't the timely voice of God Himself this very week glorify His Son in the hearing of the crowd? Overwhelmed, some said it thundered. Others felt an angel had spoken to Him. Why worry, then, about what these obviously jealous religious leaders could do?

But Christ knew only too well what was ahead. His words:

*"Truly, I say to you, you will weep and lament, but your sorrow will turn to joy. Look, just as this bread is broken … my body is to be broken for you. Take, eat, and when you break bread together remember what I have done.*

*"Even as this scarlet wine is poured out, so my blood will flow on your behalf for the forgiveness of sins … as often as you drink this cup of the new covenant, do it in remembrance of me."*

Do you remember the favor I said the King wanted from you? This is it: In the horror of the ordeal He must now face alone, Jesus did not want His sacrifice, His broken body and shed blood, to be forgotten. He wanted His followers to frequently bring to mind the immense cost required of Him to complete the work of releasing captives from Satan.

How unlike all other kings He was! What's common is to expect a ruler to ask his people to give their lives on behalf of some cause he espouses. But Jesus reversed those roles and paid the great price Himself. The favor He asks of all who bear His name is that His sacrifice never be taken for granted. In a sentence:

---

*Our King requested that we regularly remember His broken body and shed blood.*

---

Therefore, throughout His Church worldwide these elements are served to His people. But just being present at such an occasion does not ensure the believer's attitude is one of deep appreciation.

I hope you're not someone who eats the bread that's offered and drinks the cup of the Lord in an unworthy fashion—allowing your mind to wander, not even attempting in your imagination to travel back to Golgotha and watch as your King, stripped of all dignity, is brutally handled, reviled, spat upon, and lifted up to die as payment for your sin.

"To eat and drink in an unworthy manner," writes Paul, "Is to be guilty of profaning the body and blood of the Lord. Anyone who eats and drinks without discerning the body, eats and drinks judgment upon himself." Communion is always a natural time to think about the King and His Kingdom.

Regularly remembering the sacrifice of our King need not be limited to His table. From the New Testament I notice that before leaving the Upper Room, they sang a hymn together. How I thank God for the music of His Church. If your skills are as limited as mine are, maybe you should rest content to just read several hymns a day as has been my practice.

*Hail! Thou once despised Jesus!*
*Hail, thou Galilean King!*
*Thou didst suffer to release us,*
*Thou didst free salvation bring.*
*Hail, thou agonizing Savior,*
*Bearer of our sin and shame!*
*By thy merits we find favor;*
*Life is given through thy name.*

I find hymns a great help in regularly remembering our Lord's sacrifice as He requested.

Finally, when is the last time you consciously knelt in respect before your King and said, "My sole desire for an audience, your majesty, is that I might again thank you for the wounds you were willing to receive on my behalf. The stripes on your back, the punctures in your brow, the nail holes in both hands and feet, the spear laceration in your side. I thank you from the bottom of my heart for a love of which I am most unworthy."

~

*He thinks that the shadows, forms deeper than the substance of darkness, creep closer to the pyre that rises black, a rubble of twisted cinder in the middle of Burning Place. Someone stands beside him and reaches to him a hand. It is an old woman, more bent than ever, the grasp now feeble. It is Mercie.*

*"Why are they here?" he asks her, motioning to the shadows. "Must all who love him come?"*

*Her voice is weak; her answer sounds far away. "Yes. All who love the King must come to this place before they can see the Restoration begin."*

**From the *Tales of the Resistance* story:**
**"Burning Place"**

# CHAPTER 27

# A CASE OF EXPEDIENCY

~

IN A.D. 312 the Roman emperor Constantine supposedly had a vision. The sign under which he should lead his armies was the cross. Most historians see this decision as one of expediency, something that Constantine understood would best serve his interests. For Christians, however, it meant an end to the Roman persecutions.

But let's go back further to a case of expediency in the New Testament. It was the relationship of Christ the King to the Roman powers, and to do that I will focus on our Lord's trial. Actually, what we think of as a "Trial" was not at all what occurred.

On a Thursday night Jesus was taken captive in the Garden of Gethsemane. By early afternoon on Friday, a little over half a day later, He was already on the cross. In that short span of time Christ was examined by the makeshift Jewish Sanhedrin, twice by Pilate, and once by Herod. So we're not talking about what we think of as due process, trial by jury, right of appeals, and so on.

Humanly speaking, Christ's fate rested in the hands of one man—Pontius Pilate. As Roman procurator, he commanded the army of occupation in Caesarea, a Roman port on the Mediterranean in upper Palestine. He was also in charge of a detachment of troops on duty at Jerusalem and quartered next to the great temple in the Fortress Antonia. Just to be safe, when Pilate came to Jerusalem he brought additional soldiers to control the city. Pilate had the power of life and death and could reverse capital sentences passed by the Sanhedrin. In fact, all such Jewish requests for the death penalty had to be submitted to him.

To give you a feel for Pilate's authority, he also appointed the high priest and controlled the temple and its funds. The very vestments of the high priests were in his custody, and he released them only for festivals.

What kind of a person was Pilate? A good hint is in Luke 13, where some people told Christ of the Galileans whose blood Pilate mixed with their sacrifices. Also, Josephus, the ancient Jewish historian, says Pilate had used money from the temple treasury to build an aqueduct to convey water to the city from a spring some miles away. Tens of thousands of Jews had demonstrated against this when Pilate came to Jerusalem at a festival time. In retaliation, he sent his troops in disguise among them and a large number of Jews were slain.

This event presumably caused the rift with Herod spoken of in Luke 23. In the process, Pilate's men had killed some of Herod's Galilean subjects. Galilee was the territory by the Sea of Galilee where Christ had been raised as a lad. You recall after Christ's arrest, when Pilate heard Jesus was a Galilean, he sent Him over to King Herod, who was in Jerusalem at the time. Herod was the ruler who earlier had ordered John the Baptist beheaded.

So here were two rulers—both of whom had the power to do away with Christ, although surprisingly, neither was prone to judge Christ guilty. Herod, still smarting from the public's response to his crime against John, contented himself to mock our Lord by dressing Him in gorgeous royal apparel and faking worship, before returning Him to Pilate.

Uneasy himself, Pilate was not sure he wanted to tangle with this man about whom he had heard so many strange tales. Also, the issue of kingdoms made him nervous. "Are you the king of the Jews?" he asked.

The answer: "My kingship is not of this world; if my kingship or kingdom were of this world my servants would fight."

"So are you a king?!"

"For this reason I was born, and for this I have come into the world."

In John 19:1-22, the matter of kingship surfaces six times more: verses 3, 12, 14, 15, 19 and 21.

So Pilate said to the crowd, "You brought this man as one who was perverting and misleading the people, and behold, after examining him before you, I have not found any offense in this man in regard to your accusations against him; nor indeed did Herod, for he sent him back to us!"

Did you hear that? Quite an unexpected turn of events.

But wait, there's even more: "Behold, I will therefore chastise him [have him flogged] and deliver him to you having been taught his lesson [reformed], and release him."

"That's bad," you say, "prisoners often went mad under the lash with its bits of bone and jagged steel that dug out one's flesh. If He's innocent, why put Christ through that torture?"

Wait! Pilate's wife sent word to him saying, "Have nothing to do with that righteous man—for I have suffered much over him today in a dream."

But on the other side the crowd was now screaming, "Away with this man, and release to us Barabbas"—one who had been thrown into prison for an insurrection started in the city and for murder.

Pilate addressed them once more concerning his desire to release Jesus. But they shouted, "Crucify him, crucify him!"

A third time he said to them, "Why? What evil has he done?" But they were urgent, demanding with loud cries that he should be crucified.

The next sentence is short—just four words: "And their voices prevailed!"

So Pilate gave sentence that their demands should be granted. He released the man sentenced for insurrection and murder; but Jesus, the King, he delivered up to their will.

Dirty, isn't it? If Pilate felt Christ was innocent, why didn't he stick to his guns? Sure, he washed his hands, saying, "I am innocent of this man's blood, see to it yourselves." But that hardly erased his involvement in the greatest miscarriage of justice in history.

"But why?" you ask. "Pilate had the power; all he had to do was to say no!"

But you see, it wasn't the expedient thing. For Pilate to have put what he perceived as right above any personal considerations, would have resulted in him identifying with the very Son of God himself. But at the moment the procurator had an angry crowd on his hands. And not just the rabble-rousers, either. There were the Jewish religious leaders so skilled at applying "The old pressure." "If you release this man, you're not Caesar's friend," they prompted the crowd to shout.

"Everyone like this Jesus who makes himself a king sets himself against Caesar!"

All Pilate needed in his dog-eat-dog world were a few distorted reports sent to Rome saying he refused to move against a supposed activist who claimed he, not Caesar, was King and God. So Pilate succumbed to the politicians' disease—expediency. He did what was best for his own interests rather than what he perceived to be right.

For the record, just let me say politicians certainly aren't the only ones known for being adept at replacing right with what seems best at the moment for old number-one. It plays a big part in business relationships. And students face such pressures. In fact, just about anywhere there is competition, it shows up—even in church and at home.

Perhaps you face a Pilate-like decision right now, choosing between what's best for you and what's really right.

Listen. To act out of expediency is often to again render judgment against Christ Himself.

On the other hand:

---

*To put what's perceived as right above personal considerations results in identifying with God's anointed King.*

---

Maybe you're thinking, as Pilate no doubt did, *Come on now, this is just another day that involves dozens of tough decisions.*

We know what that's like. Probably in the pressure of the moment, Pilate felt his judgment was rather astute. But in terms of the future judgment he will face, with the roles reversed, few would change places with Pilate—or with anyone, for that matter, who acts in a similar fashion.

~

*"First witness," called the Clerk.*

*It was the Chief Herald, the one formerly known as Doublespeak. His friends said that he was Doublespeak no more, but Doomster, the one who pronounced judgment on behalf of the Enchanter. The emblem of the Fire Wizard was emblazoned on his elegant purple jersey; he wore brass armbands and a circlet of gold upon his head. "Why, I heard, I heard with my very own ears this man, this prisoner there, proclaim another Kingdom, where the subjects live in the light. He attempted to entice me, me, the Chief Herald to the Enchanter, to treason."*

*Someone in the courtroom called out, "Treachery!" Another shouted, "Death to pretenders!"*

**From the *Tales of the Resistance* story:**
**"Traffic Court"**

# CHAPTER 28

# COME SEE THE KING

~

"COME WITH ME. I want you to meet a great king." When I say those words, you no doubt picture yourself on a journey to another country. You might visualize a palace with an elaborate throne room where we are escorted into the presence of the monarch himself. But that's not the scene I have in mind; instead, I want to take you to a place of public execution.

"Then this king of yours must have recently lost in battle," you respond.

"No, on the contrary, he was victorious."

"I don't understand," you say.

Then let me give you some background on the way. All the world longs for a perfect king—someone with great wisdom and compassion who also has the authority and power to govern his subjects in such a way that they could truly experience the best life possible. Theoretically, if a wise and compassionate person possesses both the authority and power to govern, such a king would be ideal.

Now, the man we're going to see is just as I've described. Though young, at thirty-three his wisdom is profound. His thoughts are like a stream of fresh, clear water running through an otherwise parched countryside. And he is loving, especially when it comes to the underprivileged, the disenfranchised, and those taken advantage of.

His powers are unique also—over sickness, death, demonic forces. All of nature knows his voice and instantly obeys his commands. His authority is from on high. At the beginning of his ministry, the voice of God actually said, "Thou are my beloved Son, with thee I am well pleased."

His mission included teaching his subjects how to live. "The obedience that marks heaven and results in beauty there," he stated, "Is what should be manifested among members in my kingdom here on earth as well!"

A questioner said, "Sum up for us what it is you want us then to do."

His reply: "Love the Lord your God with all your heart, and your neighbor as yourself." What a fabulous place this world would be if everyone actually honored God with a full heart and treated fellow humans with genuine love as well! Why, if love for God and others was habitually manifested only among those who profess to bow before Him as their sovereign, this earth would be a markedly better place.

Falling short of this standard is what Scripture calls "sin." Ignoring God or paying Him token homage or stepping on neighbors to get what is desired, or loving only when there is personal benefit or love returned, we all fall miserably short of the glory of God.

Incidentally, we're on our way to the Middle East to see this king. Since there is still a little time before we arrive, let me give more background about what you'll witness.

At this time it was not the purpose of this special King from heaven to reign indefinitely here on earth. In His place, He will leave His Spirit—the Holy Spirit—who will minister to us in an unusual way. In fact, through a miracle He calls "being born anew," the Spirit will personally indwell each person who wishes to learn this life of love for God and others. The Holy Spirit within, the mark of all true believers, will then in various ways teach converts this beautiful alternative lifestyle.

You must understand, though, before one's body can become a dwelling-place of this newly assigned Counselor, the Holy Spirit, or before we can individually or corporately become a living temple for God, all sin must be removed. That's because the King is holy and unwilling to accommodate Himself to evil. Even if on our own we began to change for the good, how could we resolve the problem of past sins?

The answer is we can't—at least not on our own. Without a sinless one willing to suffer in our place the penalty of our failings, not only would we never have the privilege of experiencing this glorious Kingdom, we also would be forever banned as offenders against the Lord.

The good news, however, is that this King we are to see momentarily has chosen to take our place. There, look down, before you now, the small hill just outside the old city wall. He hangs there naked on the middle cross. Not a pretty sight, is it!

His body is bloody from the lashes given Him by the soldiers following His trial. Their leather whip was studded with sharpened pieces of bone and lead pellets. On those same blood-stained shoulders He carried the heavy cross-beam most of the way through the city. Now His hands are nailed to it. He has been hanging there in agony about three hours. Usually He remains silent, unlike the other two being crucified. For a while they railed at Him, as did a number of the spectators, including certain religious leaders.

The crown of thorns on His head was put there when the battalion of the governor's soldiers mocked Him after His beating. He sat trembling in shock as they knelt before him in contempt and said, "Hail, King of the Jews," and spat on Him and struck Him on the head.

He doesn't have to be there. In the garden, when taken captive He claimed He could have called for more than twelve legions of angels and they would have responded instantly. But He didn't, for He intended to die on our behalf. See, He's taking on himself the rightful penalty for our sins, so we in turn can be forgiven.

Many years before, Isaiah the prophet wrote: "He was wounded for our transgressions, he was bruised for our iniquities, and with his stripes we are healed. All we like sheep have gone astray, we have turned every one to his own way and the Lord has laid on him the iniquity of us all."

Said differently, He's being cut off from the Father by our sins. That's the real essence of death—separation from God.

Moments ago He cried, "My God, my God, why hast thou forsaken me?" Our disobedience—yours and mine—has now come between the Father and His special Son.

Knowing who He really is, one feels terribly torn. Without His blood being shed, there would be no forgiveness for our sins. But still this sight breaks your heart: a great King suffering because He loves His wayward subjects.

Listen. He speaks of two things before He dies: "Father, into your hands I commend my spirit." That prayer from the Psalms was the first prayer a Jewish mother taught her child to say before the dark of night came down. Then He says, "It is finished." In the Greek, I'm told this is not an expression of resignation. It's a shout of triumph. Before the unnatural darkness descends on this scene, Jesus knows He has done all He was asked to accomplish.

I hope this picture helps you understand the awfulness of sin. Why was Jesus humiliated? Because He miscalculated the reaction of the Sanhedrin to His criticisms? No. Because the swiftness of the Roman trials took Him by surprise? No. It is because He wanted to solve the problem of sin.

Which sin is your special pet? Lying, bitterness, profanity, jealousy, contempt for God's house, abuse of your body, judging, prayerlessness, refusal to help the poor, disobeying your parents, falsifying reports, shoplifting, drunkenness, greed, chronic complaining, endless arguing, cheating workers, sexual impurity, withholding love? These kind of matters are why Christ suffers at Calvary—and each of them is therefore vile.

Here is my hope:

*Standing at the great King's cross should convince us of the awfulness of sin.*

I weep for the better world He wanted but that is so seldom experienced. Today people seem so casual about standards of righteousness. Oh, how I wish my words could create an aversion to sin in at least some hearts!

You know how people respond when a word like *cancer* is mentioned. They are likely to react: "Oh, no, anything but that!" Well, that's the response I want to create in you regarding sin: "Keep it away from me!" Why? Because all such malignancies are so anathema to God that He had to give His only Son to remedy the problem.

I pray my words will result in your greater awareness of this old evil. Are you persuaded?

*Now the Enchanter's limousine, long, sleek, black, silent, draws to the edge of Burning Place. The Enchanter emerges, his eyes hot with anticipation, his robe an image of woven flame. All clear a wide path for him; none wish to touch him in his heat or feel his burning gaze.*

*But he has eyes only for one—the mauled figure tied to the stake, standing bound on the pyre above the crowd. The Fire Wizard lifts his hands, throws back his head and begins to dance in triumphant celebration. He is an ogre of glee, chortling, shooting flames, flashing now light, now dark, calling the night unto himself until the people of Enchanted City gasp for air. They choke, and the head of the sacrificial one droops lower.*

**From the *Tales of the Resistance* story:**
**"Burning Place"**

# CHAPTER 29

# RESURRECTION POWER

~

M Y WIFE AND I were once privileged to be among 200 guests invited to the White House when President Reagan first announced the funding of a National Clearing Center for information on missing and runaway children. The proceedings took place in the East Room, the largest ballroom of the White House. We felt honored to have been included.

When we got home we told our four children about the experience. "What did the president look like?" they wanted to know. "And what did he say?"

Following His resurrection, Jesus was seen by more than five hundred people. What a far greater thrill that must have been. And I rather suspect that as some people returned to their homes and told of their unique experience, these same two questions were asked: "What did He look like, Dad?" and "What did He talk about?"

I would love to know the answers given to that first question. I'm confident our Lord didn't look like the average "return-from-the-dead" figures in television and movies. There is a definite otherworldliness about such characters. Christ was not a ghostlike form with a spooky voice; Christ's resurrection appearances were not eerie or weird. If anything, they were wonderful, joyous, even tender—overwhelming maybe, but not spooky. As John explains in John 20:19-20, "On the evening of that day, the first day of the week the doors being shut where the disciples were for fear of the Jews, Jesus came and stood among them and said to them, 'Peace be with you.' When he said this he showed them his hands and his side. Then the disciples were glad when they saw the Lord."

The second question, however, concerning what the resurrected Christ talked about, is directly answered in Acts 1:3: "To them he presented himself alive after his passion by many proofs, appearing to them during forty days, and speaking of [what else!] the kingdom of God." You knew that was coming, didn't you!

What is most interesting is that even after two thousand years, this glorious resurrection power of our Lord is still available to us today. Never mind that not too many experience it; just listen to what Paul says in Ephesians 1:19-20: "That you may know—what is the immeasurable greatness of his power in us who believe according to the working of his great might which he accomplished in Christ when he raised him from the dead."

Two chapters later in the same book, Paul adds, "Now to him who by the power at work within us is able to do far more abundantly than all that we ask or think, to him be glory in the church and in Christ Jesus to all generations." Remember: "All generations" includes ours. In Philippians 3:10, Paul pens these familiar words: "That I may know him [Christ] and the power of his resurrection."

Now, I can almost hear someone say, "Those verses are great. In fact, I remember when I first thought that meant Christ's resurrection power was somehow placed in us so we could do the kind of things He did! And I'd picture myself being able to zap somebody like a spiritual faith-healer. It's funny the ideas we get in our heads!"

Well, what should I say? You see, I still believe God planted within us that same explosive power that brought His Son forth from the grave, but not so we could amaze our friends with clever tricks like those bought in a cheap novelty shop. Here, I fear, is where people get mixed up.

The point merits repeating: The power of the Resurrection doesn't relate nearly as much to performing eye-popping miracles as it does to advancing the Kingdom against the powers of the enemy. Waging warfare against the forces of hell is difficult work, which takes all the weapons at God's disposal.

In fact, as a model of spiritual power, Paul is a good example of a top-rate soldier of the Kingdom. He was repeatedly wounded only to rise and fight again. The other apostles warred against incredible odds to advance the cause of their Master, and all but one died prematurely in the fray. John, the single exception, didn't exactly live the life of a celebrity either. In Revelation 1:9 he wrote while in exile, "I John, your brother, who share with you in Jesus the tribulation and the kingdom and the patient endurance, on the island of Patmos [which is not a Mediterranean vacation spot, but a Roman penal colony!] on account of the word of God and the testimony of Jesus."

You see, resurrection power relates to spiritual warfare and the advance of the Kingdom. That's why the verse I quoted earlier ends the way it does: " … that I may know him and the power of his resurrection, and may share in his sufferings, becoming like him in his death."

The key question is, Why do I want Christ's resurrection power? For my purposes, or the King's? Do I want His power so people will be impressed with me, or so the name of Christ can be upheld and His purposes accomplished?

Let's put it in contemporary terms. Do I want His resurrection power so that within the subculture of North American Christendom my books will be bestsellers, my CDs will sell more quickly in the religious bookstores, my ministry will be on the lips of all those who are born again? Or do I want this power so that believers will stop being content with mere entertainment and will be challenged to use their God-given gifts in significant Kingdom involvement? Will I use this power to reach unbelievers, not with some watered-down easy believism, but with what it means to bow low before the King of the universe? If so, the enemy strongholds will know they are under spiritual attack by the people who love the true King. That's what resurrection power is for.

Yes, it's available. And I defy anyone to read the New Testament and the lives of the early Church leaders and say I'm wrong.

*Christ's resurrection power can be known by those who seek to advance His Kingdom.*

But why discuss resurrection power when many are not even aware there's a battle of kingdoms going on? Spiritual skirmishes are fought daily. Do you realize how many opportunities you have to pray for this resurrection power?

*"Father, today I need to know Christ's resurrection power for this Kingdom reason: I'm having lunch with a friend who's very close to transferring allegiance from darkness to light and I need the King's Spirit to be present in me."*

*"Father, today I need to know Christ's resurrection power for this Kingdom reason: I've set aside the morning for fasting and prayer and I don't want it to be wasted time."*

*"Father, today I need to know Christ's resurrection power for this Kingdom reason: I'm singing at church and I want desperately to get across the message of this song."*

*"Father, today I need to know Christ's resurrection power for this Kingdom reason: The neighbors are coming again for Bible study and we want so much to sense that you are with us the entire evening."*

Suppose you were the King—involved in a great struggle with a despicable enemy over the very souls of the people you loved—and a great power was yours to bestow on those throughout your ranks. How would you feel if it was used in ways that had little to do with the outcome of the battle but rather was focused primarily on the self-aggrandizement of the ones to whom it was issued?

Wouldn't you say, "Forget it, that person's a fool who expects such requests to be granted at a time when the eternal destiny of millions is at stake!"

I suspect our King might feel that way as well.

~

*The music quickens as the King in the center stoops and lifts an armful of flame, which shimmers and flutters in his embrace, alive. And as the dance passes, he tosses a flower to this one, to that one, until the whole moving ring is filled with brilliant light, like comets, like galaxies of orbiting moons. And Hero watches as each now becomes, not passing through the Circle of Sacred Flames, but being passed through themselves by holy light as the shining fires disappear only to shine brightly from each one's eyes.*

*Then the King, the King himself, cries to Hero, "Keeper of the Chronicle! Light?" And when he turns his face, it is then that Hero sees the mark. A scar new from the burning, a scar like his own—but not like it. It is not the Enchanter's mark, not stamped into the flesh by hot iron. It is like a flower high on the cheekbone, like a crown, like a red and perfect rose. Lifting his hand to his face, Hero discovers that the rough fleshly rim of his own scar has disappeared. The mark of branding has been forever healed.*

**From the *Tales of the Resistance* story:**
**"Burning Place"**

# CHAPTER 30

# A DREAM COME TRUE

~

NOT ALL DREAMS COME TRUE. But the one shared by Christ concerning His Kingdom will. In 1 Corinthians 15 Paul wrote, "Then comes the end, when he [Christ] delivers the kingdom to God the Father after destroying every rule and every authority and every power. For he must reign until he has put all enemies under his feet." In Revelation 11:15 we read similar words: "Then the seventh angel blew his trumpet and there were loud voices in heaven saying, 'the kingdom of the world has become the kingdom of our Lord and of his Christ, and he shall reign for ever and ever.'"

Until all is fulfilled, however,

*Christ desires that His followers remain*
*captivated by His Kingdom dream.*

To captivate means to capture the attention or affection of—as by beauty, excellence, etc. So it's a fitting word.

I believe an important part of leadership involves being able to capture people with a vision of something better than what they have experienced. If anyone was ever an example of what I'm writing about it, was our Lord. There's no doubt His preaching on the Palestinian hills about the Kingdom of God or the kingdom of heaven had everyone talking.

The Kingdom was what He spoke about most often: "He went through cities and villages preaching and bringing the good news of the kingdom of God." "The kingdom," said Christ, "Is like leaven which a woman took and hid in three measures of meal," or, "The kingdom is like a merchant in search of fine pearls," or, "The kingdom is like a net thrown into the sea gathering fish of every kind." His comparisons were many.

Now, a kingdom by definition demands a king. And Christ saw Himself as filling that role. How bold Jesus had to be to voice a message about an alternative kingdom and king in a land occupied by Rome's legions! Just as phenomenal was the way the crowds were so anxious to demonstrate their support. They were only too ready to make Christ their leader.

The problem was, they didn't understand that before He could wear His crown, Christ had to bear the cross. That's because the dream couldn't be experienced until a great price had been paid for those who chose to be ransomed. And, of course, the enemy who held them bound needed to be defeated.

Incidentally, on this point almost everyone was fooled. Many of His initial hearers believed their oppressor was Caesar. Christ knew it was Satan. He realized that political freedom is not as important as spiritual emancipation. So the Kingdom message was confusing to many. After all, weren't kings supposed to fight wars, live in palaces, wear gorgeous robes, oversee society, ensure safety throughout the realm, promote prosperity—maybe even swagger a little? But in the Kingdom Christ described, enemies were to be loved. Nice clothing was unimportant. Treasures were to be laid up in the world to come, not in this one. The greatest were instructed to act humbly, like servants. And peace was possible even in the midst of turmoil. Strange—yet there was still something overwhelmingly attractive about all this—so appealing, in fact, that it was *captivating!*

Most intriguing of all—entry into Christ's Kingdom required a second birth. Just as one was born physically, so now a spiritual birth was also necessary. "Unless one is born of water [physical] and the Spirit he cannot enter the kingdom of God," was how Jesus put it. This meant that to be part of this unfolding scene would require such a drastic change it would literally require an infusing of God's Spirit into a person—first, to bring forgiveness and cleansing from past wrongs; and second, for the Spirit to establish residency to teach new Kingdom patterns and values.

This indwelling presence of the Spirit of Christ or the Holy Spirit (Romans 8:9) was not only what marked all converts; it also served as the unifying factor that fashioned Kingdom members into a new family, the family of God. They were all brothers and sisters in the Lord and cared greatly for each other.

The very hallmark of the Kingdom, you see, was Christlike love—love for God, certainly love for fellow Kingdom members, and also love for all human beings. In this regard, the King Himself is our model.

And soon, all those who chose to become a part of that Kingdom would know whether or not Christ's vision was a pipe dream. Would their sense of peace with God remain genuine? All things being equal, did seeking first the Kingdom actually result in God providing for their daily needs as promised? Did becoming a Christian really mean inheriting fine new brothers and sisters? Would Kingdom subjects weep when some suffered and rejoice when others had good news? Did peace and joy and self-control result from following the Spirit's promptings? Did talking with God in prayer accomplish anything? Was comfort found during sorrow? Had death truly lost its sting?

My conviction is that the early Kingdom members were satisfied!

And it wasn't long before the watching world would be able to contrast the beauty of this Kingdom with the other earthly kingdoms that it knew. Those early Kingdom people were impressive! They were faithful to their marriage partners. They refused to take up arms for heathen kings. "Behold how they love each other," some people said, and, "Christians know how to die well!" The contrast was great indeed!

To be sure, this was nothing compared to what would mark society when the King Himself actually later returns in person to establish His rightful rule over all the world. Nevertheless, these people lived by faith as though Christ were alive among them, which of course He was through His Spirit. The dream was not just for the future, but whenever and wherever Christ was honored by people who bowed before Him and obeyed His will.

Who can deny that the Church in those early centuries—stirred by the messages they heard the King speak and encouraged that His words represented the truth by which the universe functions—demonstrated the Kingdom for all to see. They were the "city on the hill," "The salt that flavored the rest of society," "The leaven that made the whole loaf rise," "The light of the world," or the embodiment of the dream.

What I'm wondering, of course, is at what point did these generations of disciples cease to be stirred by the vision? I mean, who really thinks these days, as believers used to, about the importance of demonstrating before the world this simple but beautiful lifestyle of the Kingdom? Where are those Christians who actually live by faith the way they would if the King were present? Personally, I fear the dream is far from most believers' minds.

And when the great dream fades, momentum breaks down, service becomes an obligation, and all too often smaller, less-worthy objectives are established throughout the ranks.

Where are you in all this? I ask because I'm convinced that until all is fulfilled, as it will be, Christ desires His followers to remain captivated by His Kingdom dream. See, you can't really be pleased with Him and yet turned off by what He was excited about.

"I have a dream." When leaders make such claims, they are calling for more than mere mental agreement. Even applause is an inadequate response. What's expected is full identification, active involvement, even sacrifice. If these aren't rendered, little more than pleasing words have been experienced. But words are hardly the stuff of which great dreams are made.

That's the reason I wrote this book. I haven't even begun to say all I should. But it's a start.

I leave you with the dream of our great King—a wonderful dream, which in one sense will come true regardless of whether or not we believe in it. But then again, it's a dream we can know even now—know personally, know corporately—depending upon what we choose to allow to capture us.

Some good people set their affection on money, sports, travel, family, theater, hobbies, music, houses, popularity—none of which in themselves is necessarily bad. Some will set their affections on these—devote most or all of their free time to them. But what about you?

> *Rise up, O men of God! Have done with lesser things:*
> *Give heart and soul and mind and strength to serve the King of Kings.*

Don't just sing about it—***live*** it!

> *We worship thee Lord Christ, our Saviour and our King,*
> *To thee our youth and strength adoringly we bring.*
> *So fill our hearts, that men may see*
> *Thy life in us, and turn to thee.*

Will you be captivated by the dream of your King? Will you shout, "Jesus, what captures my heart—captures me—is 'thy kingdom come, thy will be done on earth as it is in heaven.' I share your Kingdom dream!"?

You'll not be disappointed—in His present reign or in His kingship yet to be.

~

*The boy felt stupid. The answer seemed obvious, but he still didn't understand. "I thought this was a park."*

*"Of course it is; it's Great Park. And the Kingdom is in it. This is where the King rules in exile. But the Kingdom is not only here. It is anywhere the King is and is obeyed. Someday the King's rule will be restored in Enchanted City—and everywhere. That's why we call out, 'to the King! To the Restoration!'"*

**From the *Tales of the Kingdom* story:**
**"The Faithless Ranger"**

*The Kingdom Comes* references the *Tales of the Kingdom Trilogy* (36 stories in three books) which is available in various enhanced formats, including two illustrated hardback editions that you can enjoy reading with your kids or family:

The Classic Edition:

The Anniversary Edition:

You can order these online at Amazon or at our official website at www.KingdomTales.com. Or call Mainstay Ministries toll-free at 1-800-224-2735 to order by telephone.

www.ingramcontent.com/pod-product-compliance
Lightning Source LLC
Chambersburg PA
CBHW060927040426
42445CB00011B/828